In a day filled with self-promotio
us to what the Bible declares repeatedly from start to finish—choose and cultivate humility for a lifetime. Pat pulls back the curtain of his own heart by telling his own story of learning humility by repeatedly experiencing humiliation. Oh, if we heed the example and warning of Pat's own testimony, we might head into some of our most effective days of ministry, for His glory!

> —Brad Bigney
> Lead Pastor, Grace Fellowship Church
> Author, *Gospel Treason*
> Florence, Kentucky

At a time when so many views about Christian leadership are jaded, Pat humbly shares the wisdom of one who has grown in the knowledge of Christ for nearly 40 years. His thoughts and biblical reflections will encourage parents who are broken-hearted over their concerns for adult children, serve as a model for leaders of every age, and offer hope to those who are grieving.

> —Dr. Chris Brauns
> Pastor, The Red Brick Church
> Author, *Unpacking Forgiveness*
> Stillman Valley, Illinois

This is a timely publication. Timely, because the virtue of heart humility is rare. As Christians, we must continually cultivate it, because we are so easily puffed up by the slightest of compliments. *Retractions: Cultivating Humility* After *Humiliation* is written with refreshing honesty—but it also displays a maturity that could only come from life experiences. That's what makes this book pure gold. May God use it to be a blessing to many.

> —Ray Comfort
> Founder and CEO, Living Waters

Pat and I came to know Christ within a few months of each other. The cosmic joke is that we would both become pastors, proclaiming the gospel we once spurned and were then gloriously conquered by. I read each of these chapters with laughter, then wincing, then with tears, and always with deep gratitude for the grace that has poured over Pat. Only a life well-lived in the light of Christ can write chapters like these. "Take up and read," dear reader.

—Jeff Dodge
Teaching Pastor, Veritas Church
Assistant Professor of Theological Studies, MBTS
Iowa City, Iowa

Some biblical truths are easier to understand with flesh and blood examples. Pat's openness about his sins and mistakes from his time as a new believer to the present as a husband, father, and influential pastor are striking. Many of us have never known a respected Christian leader to be so vulnerable or heard about how God's grace and exaltation followed humiliation.

—Randy Patten
President, TEAM Focus Ministries
Director of Training Emeritus, Association of Certified Biblical Counselors

When you wrap up the last page and can't wait to read the book again, recommending it to everyone you know, you understand you're holding something that's extraordinarily special. My dear friend, Pat Nemmers, has crafted a true masterpiece. Retractions is real, raw, refreshing, and brutally authentic. As it leads you down the path of self-examination, it brings you to the brink of brokenness, and then breathes life and hope back into you again.

—Emeal ("E.Z.") Zwayne
President, Living Waters

Over the years, it has been my privilege to have a front row seat, watching God take one of the most passionate people I have ever met and cultivate humility through humbling him. *The content of this book points to the character of the man—a man of God who I am thankful to call mentor, brother in Christ, fellow soldier, and friend.* There is a friend that sticks closer than a brother—Pat is that friend to me. I encourage you to take to heart what he has written for us in this book.

—Dave Heisterkamp
Lead Pastor, Lakeside Fellowship Church
Polk City, Iowa

One of the hallmarks of humility is a willingness to be a lifetime learner. Pat will share what he has learned over his life about humility and what God used to teach him. You will be forced to consider how you have responded to situations God sent your way to humble you. Pat will highlight that due to God's grace, it is never too late to repent, seek forgiveness, and go on serving God. In living color Pat will illustrate James 4:6, "God resists the proud but gives grace to the humble." You will be encouraged and challenged by his clear examples. Well worth the read.

—Dr. Jim Tillotson
President, Faith Baptist Bible College and Theological Seminary
Ankeny, Iowa

I wish I could have read this BEFORE starting ministry! I've often said, "Pat Nemmers is who I want to be when I grow up." He's different! Not awkward or weird, but a rare breed of authenticity, with life lessons that touch the heart. Read this, and you'll recognize the humiliation, laugh with identification, and cry with appreciation. Pat meets us in failure, removes shame and regret, and delivers us to Christ to learn humility from The Master.

—Dr. Matt Shackelford
Lead Teaching Pastor, Central Church
Collierville, Tennessee

I was both nodding knowingly and rapidly taking notes as I read Pat's book. American evangelicalism is dealing with a parade of fallen leaders who seemed to value branding more than character. That means we desperately need the kind of self-effacing reflection found on these pages. Pastor Nemmers unflinchingly takes us into the darkest nights of his soul—and his most embarrassing tilts at windmills—as a service to church leaders everywhere. I applaud this veteran pastor for skipping the late-career victory lap in favor of confessing his mistakes so that others can avoid some of them.

—Trevor Meers

Board President, Freedom for Youth Ministries;

Deacon, Saylorville Church

Retractions by Pat Nemmers is real and honest. It gives us a transparent and raw look into his life and situations that God used to humble and transform him. I found myself wanting to read the next chapter and see what lesson he had learned. It made me laugh and cry. It challenged me to own my mistakes and be quick to humble myself. It was like sitting around the living room listening to my grandpa share stories about life and God's faithfulness. A great read for everyone and especially those in ministry.

—Abe Miller

Pastor of Administration, Saylorville Church

RETRACTIONS

RETRACTIONS

Cultivating Humility

After Humiliation

PAT NEMMERS

credo
house publishers

To Abe Miller,
whose boldness has saved me from
making this a four-volume series.

CONTENTS

CHAPTER 10

CHAPTER 11

CHAPTER 12

CULTIVATING HUMILITY AFTER HUMILIATION

T he idea for this book grew during a ministry trip to Oregon in 2010. My wife, Marilyn, and I were invited to speak at a conference for pastors and missionaries at beautiful Cannon Beach, located on the Pacific Ocean, where the world-famous Haystack Rock towers 235 feet above the ocean's edge.

Normally, I would have been giddy about the prospect of traveling to such a beautiful place and speaking at this venue. What a blessing to address a large group of fellow pastors and missionaries.

Besides, we love traveling, especially to places we have never experienced.

This time, however, was different. The only reason we packed our bags was that two years earlier I had committed to speak to a northwestern network of pastors. In fact, apart from this commitment made years before, I had turned down every other speaking invitation offered to me in 2010.

Let me give some context to that decision. I became a Christian in 1982. My instant zeal for Christ, the subject of my first chapter, placed me in many churches and pulpits early on. I entered full-time ministry in late 1986, before I had even graduated from Bible college. A little country church in northern Iowa sought me out, and I preached there each weekend during my senior year. Every Friday afternoon, my wife and I packed up our two kids and stuffed them into our gold 1980 Mazda RX 7, then traveled two hours north from Ankeny to a tiny, unincorporated group of homes and a grain elevator near Clarion, Iowa. We ministered throughout the weekend, then made our way back to our apartment near the Bible college on Monday. Crazy, but we loved it.

By 2010 and the trip to Cannon Beach, I had 24 years of pastoring under my belt with 12 years of service in my second church. Along the way, I had experienced a few life-altering moments that would forever shape my life, ministry, and—most importantly—my walk with God. During those years God blessed us with five more children before I was widowed. I then remarried, increasing my family from seven to ten children. At this point, three of them were married, and we even had a few grandchildren.

The church I currently pastor was experiencing tremendous growth, including reproducing ourselves through church planting. Folks were coming to Jesus, getting baptized, and growing in their faith. But at such an exciting time in ministry, all was not well with our two youngest boys, then 15 and 17 years of age. Amid incredible joy externally, I endured the dark night of the soul internally. Our boys were not only uninterested in spiritual things but were growing antagonistic to all things Christian—and to us as parents. They were constantly getting into trouble, and the high school principal and I were becoming friends for all the wrong reasons. In fact, like a friend, he would call me at virtually all hours of the day!

When my real friends asked how they could be praying for me, I had no hesitation in my response: "Pray that my sons would be converted—whatever converted means." It was not as though I didn't understand what it meant to be converted. I had certainly seen real conversion played out in my own life, as well as in those of many others, but these boys both claimed to be Christians. As it turned out, one was a Christian and the other was not, making it the perfect prayer request.

The Lord used the younger of the two to break me, starting with his arrest for assault. Then one night he decided not to come home. During that time God revealed to me an idol in my own heart I hadn't even known existed. The experience brought me to my knees and became the seed thought behind this book. I'll tell you about it in the chapter simply titled "John."

During that awful time with our boys, my wife and I made the trip to Oregon. With heavy hearts, we prepared to minister to those fellow pastors and missionaries. I had no idea how the Lord was about to use our experience at this conference to begin a process that would profoundly change me.

Regarding my feelings at the time of the trip, I am reminded of John Wesley's words as he and his brother Charles returned to England in 1735 after a failed attempt to reach the Native Americans in the northeastern frontier. He wrote, "I went to America to convert the Indians; but, oh, who shall convert me?" In my case, I was going to Oregon to minister to the hearts of pastors and missionaries— *but, oh, who would minister to my breaking heart?*

The answer, I soon discovered, was not in the form of a *who* but of a *what*. What ministered to my broken heart was the open admission not only of *who* I was but of *where* I was in life in terms of our struggle with our sons. I opened up to my peers about God's current work, not just in my ministry but in my home and heart while on the cusp of losing my very own sons.

My experience isn't worthy to be compared to that of the Wesley boys. On the other hand, it was *mine* and would set me on a course unlike anything I'd ever before experienced. I was beginning to learn how to walk humbly in the midst of humiliation.

Marilyn and I decided on our way to the conference that we would open up to our peers. We were already low; what was the worst thing that could happen? They could kick us to the curb, but we didn't think they would. We sensed that this would be a safe place to share our hearts. After all, these were our comrades in arms. Surely some of them could relate.

We had no idea.

On the second day I shared a message titled "Don't Waste Your Sins" (a variation on John Piper's book titled *Don't Waste Your Life*). My idea for the message (and the idea behind this book) came from David's incredibly humble and immortalized confession in Psalm 51. Amazingly, in a book of the Bible renowned for its exaltation of God, there are no fewer than 35 first-person pronouns throughout Psalm 51. These 35 uses of pronouns rendered in English as "me," "my," and "I" led me to this thought: *The only time to put me first is when confessing my sin.*

> **THE ONLY TIME TO PUT ME FIRST IS WHEN CONFESSING MY SIN.**

Adding to that, the inscription to the psalm has David turning it over to his choirmaster to be sung by those assembling to worship! Here is the opening inscription: "To the choirmaster,

A Psalm of David, when Nathan the prophet went to him, after he had gone into Bathsheba." In essence, God told David, "This song is a recording of your confession (not your sin), and I'm putting it in My inspired book for everyone to see and read for all eternity!"

And that's exactly what God did.

The thought then occurred to me, *If David could relive his past humiliation, I could testify of my current one.*

And that's exactly what *I* did.

The result was a new freedom I had not felt in years; it required deep openness, with admission of personal sin and flat-out foolish thinking on my part. We also experienced an unexpected response from our fellow servants of Christ. As we opened up about our struggles over our boys, these pastors and missionaries began to open up about their own wayward kids. One woman approached us in tears, confessing that this was the first time a conference had afforded her and her husband permission to share the struggles they were having with a daughter. Others openly acknowledged that they, too, had children going through similar circumstances. Some of their kids had recovered spiritually and were now walking with God. Their stories helped encourage those of us whose hearts were hurting in the moment. Through our tears of confession, we were given hope. We realized that we would not have received that hope had we withheld our humiliation.

So, what is the aim of this book? That you will see both God and yourself: when we see God more clearly, we see ourselves more clearly. Then, and only then, can we make the necessary adjustments going forward in life. This is exactly what happened to Job, who, after insisting that God grant him an audience in order that he might defend himself, finally got his answer. God granted him that audience. Envision this scene: "Then the LORD answered Job out of the whirlwind and said: 'Who is this that darkens counsel by words without knowledge? Dress for action like a man; I will question you, and you make it known to me'" (Job 38:1–3).

In other words, "You are questioning *Me*? No. Get your act together, Job, because I'm going to question *you!*" God would then reveal Himself to Job through a dazzling display of His awesome power, transporting him back to when He had created the universe and its constellations, the world and its weather systems, and even referring to His provision for the animal world, asking the rhetorical question, "Where were you when I did all this?"

> SO, WHAT IS THE AIM OF THIS BOOK? THAT YOU WILL SEE BOTH GOD AND YOURSELF: WHEN WE SEE GOD MORE CLEARLY, WE SEE OURSELVES MORE CLEARLY.

Job, having caught but a glimpse of God's inexhaustible power and wisdom, finally spoke up: "Behold, I am of small account; what shall I answer you? I lay my hand on my mouth. I have spoken once, and I will not answer; twice, but I will proceed no further" (Job 40:4–5). Job saw himself as a speck in God's sight. So dumbstruck was he by what he had witnessed that he basically said, "I'm done talking."

God, however, wasn't done. He reminded Job of his audacity in questioning God's wisdom. He then took Job on a detailed examination of two of His most majestic creatures—an examination that would have made the producers of *Animal Planet* stand in awe.

The realization brought Job to repentance. "I had heard of you by the hearing of the ear, but now my eye sees you; therefore I despise myself, and repent in dust and ashes" (Job 42:5–6). What changed? Job did—when he saw himself before God and God before himself. Job's story survives and will survive for all eternity so that the rest of us can learn from his humbling experience.

Though we aren't Job-like, all of us have humbling experiences designed by God to shape our lives. However, my experience from many years of working with people is that most of us, once we have confessed and forsaken our sin, wish the whole thing (including the memories) would all go away. My plea to you in this book is, "Don't do that!" Instead of wasting your sin, let the many people near and dear to you learn from your humility to prayerfully avoid your pitfall.

In this book I will point out the life lessons God has taught and is still teaching me, focusing on several personal blunders along the way. My hope is to inspire you in your walk with God by showing how faithful He has been to me despite my many failures. If you're in ministry, I hope you'll appreciate the struggle involved in change and discover that humility is required in order for us to acknowledge those changes needed in our life. If you are a lay servant in your church or community, these lessons will encourage you, too.

I've served as a pastor for over thirty years in two different churches. While experiencing the joy of considerable growth, I'll acknowledge that I'm not leading a mega church. We are closer to a thousand than to ten thousand in attendance. We have started six churches, not thirty. In the words of William Carey, "I can plod."[1]

My prayer is that this book will help you to plod along, too—in humility even, and perhaps especially, after humiliation.

RETRACTIONS

The book is titled *Retractions*,[2] and this is my working definition: an honest, humble look at past (and some current) ways of thinking and acknowledgment of my errors in them. Retraction for any of us entails a willingness to openly admit, confess, and repent of our errors and to *keep confessing them*—not only for our own benefit but also for the benefit of others. It's about cultivating humility *after* being humbled.

When I first told our staff that I was thinking of writing this book, with the idea of addressing things I'd said or done and regretted, one of the guys responded, "Will this be volume one?"

We'll see.

To help you take a few moments to contemplate the retractions I share, I've included a section for personal reflection at the end of each chapter, titled "Cultivating Humility."

Retractions. Are you open to making a few? Then join me on my own journey to forgiveness, freedom, and the joy of ongoing humility.

Pat Nemmers

CHAPTER 1

ZEAL WITHOUT KNOWLEDGE

Desire without knowledge is not good.

PROVERBS 19:2

agree with the old saying "I'd rather tone down a fanatic than heat up a corpse." Uninspiring and unmotivated leaders are hard to follow. We want our leaders to have zeal, energy, and conviction. Abraham Lincoln once said, "I don't like to hear cut and dried sermons. No—when I hear a man preach, I like to see him act as if he were fighting bees!"[3]

Without a doubt, there is a place for men who, by their God-given, Holy Spirit-driven energy, inspire God's people to respond to the message of His Word. But for all their positive energy and the joy they bring, there is the danger of acting in zeal without knowledge. Solomon put it well: "Desire without knowledge is not good, and whoever makes haste with his feet misses his way" (Proverbs 19:2). Later, Paul describes Israel's blindness as coming not from lack of fervor but from lack of knowledge:

Brothers, my heart's desire and prayer to God for [Israel] is that they may be saved. For I bear them witness that they have a zeal for God, but not according to knowledge. For, being ignorant of the righteousness of God, and seeking to establish their own, they did not submit to God's righteousness (Romans 10:1–3).

How tragic! Both Old and New Testament writers point out how zeal, a quality God intends to inspire and direct His people, can become dangerous (the Hebrew word in Proverbs 19 conveys danger) and is capable of leading others into an acceptance of false teaching.

Young men seem to be especially susceptible to this line of thinking. Too often, they are driven by their zeal *for* God but lack the knowledge *of* God needed to fuel that zeal. Revivalist Leonard Ravenhill used to describe these zealots as "three miles wide and three inches deep."

Lieutenant General George Armstrong Custer, an iconic figure of the American West, is known primarily for his ignominious death at his infamous stand at Little Big Horn. Historians debate exactly how the debacle came to an end because none of Custer's troops lived to tell about it! What is documented, besides his huge ego, is Custer's long history of rushing pell-mell into battle. As Custer rode out to his demise, one officer, knowing Custer's habit of waiting for no one, called out to him, "Now Custer, don't be greedy, but wait for us." "No, I will not,"[4] Custer replied as he rode off.

As it turned out, the 7th Cavalry faced perhaps the largest gathering of Native American warriors ever assembled on the Great Plains. Further, Custer's lack of coordination with the troops he had divided up for the coming battle would leave him and his 261 men by themselves, unprotected and defenseless. No one survived. Surely, "desire without knowledge is not good, and whoever makes haste . . . misses his way."

In the New Testament, the book of Acts tells the story of Apollos, a man I can relate to. Notice Paul's description:

> He was an eloquent man, competent in the Scriptures. He has been instructed in the way of the Lord. And being fervent in spirit, he spoke and taught accurately the things concerning Jesus, though he knew only the baptism of John. He began to speak boldly in the synagogue (Acts 18:24–26).

Apollos, a zealous man on fire for Christ, had knowledge that was accurate but incomplete. When an older couple heard him, they were immediately struck by two things: Apollos's passion for Christ and his need for clarity in his teaching. The text goes on to say, "They took him aside and explained to him the way of God more accurately" (Acts 18:26). The Greek word rendered "accurately" carries the idea of *exactness*.

I, like Apollos, learned early on that my zeal for Jesus did not make up for my lack of exactness. As a preacher, I was like the proverbial bull in a china shop. I can still be bullish at times, but I am learning how not to break the china! The Lord used a couple of watershed moments to cut deeply into my heart and life as a young preacher; both are embarrassing to recall, but both need to be shared.

My unfettered zeal began the moment I became a Christian. The errors of the church I was raised in so appalled me that I was ready to make a beeline to my parents to confront them.

My older brother, who led me to Christ, lovingly cautioned me against going. He used a silly analogy that nonetheless arrested my attention: "Pat, if you go there now, without the ability to accurately share biblical truth, you'll be like a cowboy going to a gunfight with an unloaded gun." My brother stepped in and stopped a confrontation that would have showcased my limited knowledge of God and His Word. Instead, I hunkered down to earnestly read my Bible and memorize key biblical passages. I quickly discovered that zeal tethered to truth is a powerful and compelling combination.

> I QUICKLY DISCOVERED THAT ZEAL TETHERED TO TRUTH IS A POWERFUL AND COMPELLING COMBINATION.

HOLDING MY GROUND

A week or so after my conversion, my wife and I were attending a party where there was a lot of drinking. By that time I had memorized exactly one verse: "I am the way, the truth and the life. No man comes to the Father except through me" (John 14:6). During the party my best friend, who had been the best man at our wedding, called me over to settle an argument he was having with his fiancé: "Pat, tell Sue what church we should get married in. She thinks we should marry in her church, and I say we should marry in mine." I didn't realize it at the time, but God was preparing me for my real calling—to preach the gospel with both zeal *and* knowledge.

Armed with what little knowledge I had of the churches my friend and his fiancé attended, I instantly responded, "I wouldn't get married in either one of them if they didn't preach the gospel." I couldn't believe the words that had just come out of my mouth, and I quickly took the opportunity to quote John 14:6: "Jesus said to him, 'I am the way, and the truth, and the life. No one comes to the Father except through me.'"

They were stunned. In fact, they probably thought I had been kidnapped by aliens and was being held captive somewhere else because the guy they were talking to was definitely not Pat Nemmers. Part of that was true—I was a new creation in Christ (2 Corinthians 5:17).

Suddenly, it was game on. They began to challenge me by citing one group of people in the world after another.

"What about the Muslims? Don't you think they're going to heaven?" I replied with John 14:6.

"How 'bout the Hindus?"

John 14:6.

"What about the dedicated nuns of Roman Catholicism?"

John 14:6.

"Our dedicated, hard-working friends?" (They actually named one.)

Same reply? Yep. John 14:6.

We went from the party to a restaurant, still debating. I knew only one verse by heart, and I held them off with it for three hours!

Now, admittedly, one verse is not much, but each word is full of truth. I remember thinking something along the lines of *Wow! If one verse is this powerful, I wonder how effective I'd be with two or three under my belt!*

A few months later I left for Bible college to pursue a pastoral degree. During my first semester, I commuted with two other guys for the two-hour trip one-way. They were mature Christians, and I welcomed the opportunity to converse with them on all things spiritual twice a week with eight hours of road time. One morning, as we were making our way through the countryside on our way to school, I made a zealous comment about what the Bible has to say on a certain subject. To my surprise, one of the guys asked me where the truth I so confidently declared was to be found in the Bible. I can still remember holding my Bible and sheepishly replying, "I don't know for sure, but I know it's in here somewhere!" Clearly, my answer did not impress him. He might have been driving, but that didn't stop him from sternly looking my way and stating, "Nemmers, don't you ever tell me something the Bible says unless you can give me a book, chapter, and verse."

Stunned, and maybe a little irritated, I acknowledged to myself that I had thought what I said to be true. Why did he need to be so hard on me? In reality, he had done me a favor—a great favor. In fact, that moment became a true milestone in my life. Sitting in the car and staring out the window, I realized again that my zeal was not being matched with knowledge. From that front passenger's seat, I vowed never to make another confident statement about what God's Word declared unless I could go to the very passage where it was taught. From that life-changing moment, I began a course that would combine my zeal with humility and knowledge.

HOW OUR ZEAL CAN BLIND US

The key word in that last sentence is "began." I *began* to combine my zeal with humility and knowledge. The nature of zeal is to run ahead of those things. If you, like me, are a zealous person by nature, get ready for more than a few lessons along the way.

Sharing this lesson grieves me, yet I'm convinced that I need to because it reveals the immature, hard, blinded-by-zeal, and just plain ungodly thinking that sometimes dominated my life as a young pastor. Some of you might find this story to be more of a challenge than a testimony. If this does challenge you, you have your own soul searching to do.

CONSEQUENCES OF DISOBEDIENCE

Before I tell you my own story, let me refer to a story in the Old Testament of a young prophet who had been given a specific task that unfolded in flamboyant fashion. He confronted an ungodly king in front of an ungodly altar and prophesied about the coming of a godly king. The ungodly king was enraged and called for the young prophet to be seized and punished. As the king pointed angrily at the prophet, his finger, along with his entire hand, immediately withered. The altar then split in two, just as the prophet had said it would, leaving the ungodly king reduced to tears and begging the prophet for mercy.

How cool! All in a day's work. Job well done. God is exalted. Time to go home.

Except that the young prophet didn't go directly home, as God had commanded. He delayed his leaving, spending time with an old prophet he had just met, which led to his being killed by a lion when he finally started for home. The epitaph given by the old prophet as he stared at the younger prophet's mangled body is sobering. He eulogized him as "the man of God who disobeyed the word of the LORD" (1 Kings 13:26).

Ugh—now my story:

The first church I pastored sat in the middle of nowhere, in northern Iowa. Holmes, the name of this former town, had once had its own post office, but now it melded into another small town three miles to the west. Holmes consisted of a grain elevator, maybe six or seven houses, and two churches. I pastored the little, conservative Baptist church right next door to a more liberal church. In fact, our parking lots literally ran together with nothing separating them.

In those days I was a Christian first, but I was also a Baptist. A Baptist Christian—*Baptist*, with a capital *B*. That means I stood for all things Baptist and against most things associated with the church next door. We had some areas of theological agreement with them, but our differences were simply a bridge too far. To be clear, our theological differences with this particular church were just too great to permit us to have fellowship with the people worshipping there. Theirs was not a gospel-preaching church, and they were liberal in most areas of theology.

But we were neighbors. We were still obligated to love and respect each other. In fact, legend has it that many years prior to my coming, a trench had been dug and an electrical wire laid down between the two churches. Should one church need to use the other's facilities as an overflow for a big wedding or funeral, the wire would allow the service to be piped over, allowing additional people to listen in. I never found any evidence of that wire, but if I had I might have had it cut. I didn't have any personal vendettas with anyone in that church, but I held the position of being a strong separatist. By that I mean that I severed spiritual ties with people or churches that didn't hold to the theological positions I embraced. Separation *can* harden those who take the position, but, to be fair, not all separatists are hard and cold toward those of different faiths. I have many friends within that movement who would be aghast at finding out what I did.

In any case, this is not about taking a strong position on separation. This is about a young pastor whose zeal took him much too far and, as a result, did real damage to his testimony and to that of his church for years to come. All of this happened because I chose a prayer meeting over an act of kindness.

NOT LOVING MY NEIGHBOR

Not long before I came to pastor the little Baptist church, the liberal church next door caught fire and burned down. By the time I arrived, a beautiful new church had been built, and the congregation announced it was having an open house. Of course, they sent our church an invitation, but I not only ignored the invitation but forbade the leadership of my church to attend!

Wait—it gets worse.

The night of the open house was also the night of our weekly Bible study and prayer meeting. I arrived early to conduct the service and was stunned by the masses of people attending the open house. Not only was the new church parking lot full, but the well-wishers had taken up nearly half of *our* parking lot. I thought, *The nerve of these people—that church. Surely, they knew we had services on this night.*

Our parking lot could hold about 45 cars, and they had around 20 cars parked in our lot. That would leave room for at least 25 cars for our church family to park. No problem, right? Wrong. Forget the fact that we were lucky if 10 cars made it out to prayer meeting; there was a principle at stake here. They were parking in *our* parking lot without permission and taking up so much space we would only have 15 spaces left by the time all our folks got there!

You can see where this is going. This thoughtless move on their part would not do. So, I marched over to the new church, with its open house in progress, and quietly yet firmly informed the ushers that our prayer meeting was about to start and their visitors were filling up our parking lot. In seconds, those ushers were grabbing keys from the vehicle owners and running out the door of their church. Within five minutes they had moved every single one of those cars and squeezed them into their parking lot.

As they were still moving the cars, it dawned on me what I had done. I remember thinking, *Oh, man—I hope our people show up tonight*. By the time the ushers had moved all their cars, our own folks, utterly oblivious to what had happened, started showing up for church. Sure enough, we filled up our normal eight to ten spaces. I can still picture in my mind's eye: the new church parking lot overflowing with cars out to the highway, with our own church parking lot right beside it, empty except for a handful of cars. There I stood, blinded by duty, emptied of love, and now wearied with shame.

> THERE I STOOD, BLINDED BY DUTY, EMPTIED OF LOVE, AND NOW WEARIED WITH SHAME.

This was another moment for which I would pay to get a "do-over," but we rarely get those, do we? The only thing I could do was confess my shameful action, ask God to forgive me, and vow never again to let something like this happen.

The retraction for me was, with God's help, to never let my theological beliefs interfere with the call of God to "love your neighbor as yourself." That's good, practical theology, but it wasn't my theology then. Thankfully, I had the privilege of pastoring that little Baptist church for many more years, and, slowly, I established a more Christlike testimony with our neighbor next door. My prayer is to never again allow my zeal for the things that differentiate my own faith from another's to get in the way of an opportunity to love my neighbor.

CULTIVATING HUMILITY

Zeal can be a good thing when grounded in the truth, but it can also be spiritually blinding, misdirecting our drive and passion. Scripture speaks about people who were blinded by zeal. Peter cut off a man's ear in his misdirected zeal (Luke 22:50), and Paul acknowledged his own zeal prior to salvation:

> For you have heard of my former life in Judaism, how I persecuted the church of God violently and tried to destroy it. And I was advancing in Judaism beyond many of my own age among my people, *so extremely zealous was I* for the traditions of my fathers (Galatians 1:13–14, emphasis mine).

Later, Paul reminds us that even Law-abiding Jews "have a zeal for God, but not according to knowledge" (Romans 10:2).

Zeal is a double-edged sword. My youthful zeal in quoting John 14:6 to my friends proved to be very effective. I learned the power of God's Word even when I knew only one verse by heart. Sadly, I also learned how my zeal for a sparsely attended church meeting, combined with my sense of duty to keep *our* parking lot clear for *our* people, ruined an opportunity to show love and kindness to our neighboring church family as they celebrated their new building.

Zeal must be welded to knowledge and humility. If you are a zealous person by nature, you have even more motivation to remain humble while growing in knowledge before both God and people.

Has there been a time when your zeal took you too far? When? What did you do? Did you burn a bridge unnecessarily? Could you still repair it?

It's always hard to admit it when our thinking and actions are immature. But be encouraged. After all, don't the commands to "grow in grace" (2 Peter 3:18) and to "go on to maturity" (Hebrews 6:1) imply that we haven't yet arrived? Be encouraged that God expects us to fail from time to time, . . . but be humble when you do. God also expects us to go on and grow up in our faith, while tethering our zeal to knowledge and humility.

SCRIPTURES FOR MEDITATION

Proverbs 19:2; Matthew 15:8–9; Luke 9:49–56;
and 1 Corinthians 13:11.

CHAPTER 2

HOW TO EAT CROW

"The best time to eat crow is when it's young and tender."

On Mother's Day 1986, I preached my first message in the little country church I would later come to pastor. Before I tell you what happened that day, I need to set the stage from one year earlier. A fellow Bible college student, Brad, and I were working the third shift at UPS, and we carpooled with a man named Nick. We zealously shared the gospel with him every night, five days a week. In fact, we worked every evangelistic angle we could think of; though he showed interest, it didn't go any farther. Finally, one night on the way to work, Brad and I described Jesus as the culmination of the sacrificial system of the Old Testament. Nick interrupted us by blurting out, "You two make Jesus out to be a scapegoat!" My buddy, who was sitting in the backseat, could hardly contain himself. He literally leaped forward, bouncing against the front seat, and yelled, "Yes! Yes! That's exactly Who Jesus is—your scapegoat!" I cannot describe the incredible power of the moment. Nick was instantly struck by the power of the analogy he himself had unwittingly invoked. After we pulled into the UPS parking lot, he humbly received Jesus as Savior and Lord. A few weeks later, Nick's wife also came to Jesus.

Fast forward one year. Nick took a farmhand job in northern Iowa, and he and his young family began attending a little Baptist church in the countryside. Desiring to be baptized, he invited my friend Brad and me to come witness their declaration of faith. As it turned out, the little church was without a pastor. When the deacons discovered my connection to their young convert, they invited me to come back again to preach.

Now, back to Mother's Day. I was preparing the first message I would ever preach in the church, and it was going to be a Mother's Day message for the ages. That's the thing about young zealots. They think every message they preach will be one for the ages! I chose the story of Hannah and Samuel from 1 Samuel 1–2. After covering the miraculous circumstances surrounding the birth of Samuel, I noted that, when the boy was just three years of age, Hannah kept her promise to give her son back to God; she took him to the temple and gave him into the care of Eli, the high priest. Toward the end of my message, I astounded the congregation with my explanation of the chapter's final verse, which reads, "Therefore I have lent him to the LORD. As long as he lives, he is lent to the LORD. *And he worshiped the LORD there*" (1 Samuel 1:28, emphasis mine).

I cried out, "Did you see that? The last phrase says that Samuel—at age three—*worshipped* the Lord! Is that even possible? How does a three-year-old worship God unless he knows God? I submit to you that God had made little Samuel's heart so sensitive that he had come to know God at a very young age."

I then shared the illustration of a recent event when my own three-year-old daughter had trusted in Christ. I explained that, a few weeks earlier, we'd had friends from out of town staying with us. We debated how old a child needed to be before having the capacity (humanly speaking) to trust in Jesus. I declared to my friends with great certainty that too many kids make false professions at an early age and then go through life thinking they are saved, when, in fact, they are not.

While this is true, an event that took place the very next morning did little to verify my diatribe. Early the next day our three-year-old, who had been very tender to spiritual things for some time, approached her mother and me with a picture of a heart she had drawn in pencil on a little piece of spiral notebook paper. She told us she had Jesus in her heart now. I was incredulous, to say the least. She then led us into her bedroom, knelt next to her bed, and reenacted what she had done the previous evening. Our little girl prayed again, confessing her sin and placing her faith in Jesus. She had done the same thing already the night before— on the very night I had confidently declared that too many little ones make false professions.

Game. Set. Match. After that perfect illustration, my message had nothing left but the invitation. I applied the truth that godly moms and dads can expect their little ones who have heard the gospel message from childhood to be saved at a very young age—just like Samuel.

Again, this was the very first message I ever preached in the little country church that would soon become my first pastorate, lasting nearly a dozen years. The people were moved, some to tears. They could hardly wait for me to return for the evening service later that day.

GEORGE

George was one of the senior saints I met that morning. He was nearly eighty years old, and I later came to appreciate his depth. His layman's knowledge and handling of the Scriptures were simply astounding. When he prayed publicly, he was so caught up in worshipping the Lord that he almost appeared to be in a trance. He literally prayed Scripture with a natural joy and reverence that I'd never heard from anyone else. Truthfully, I would have had him pray to close out every service, were it not for three or four other heavyweight champions of the faith we had in our little church. They were all godly men, though none other so reverent as George.

I walked into the church that Mother's Day evening still riding high on the morning's experience and strode right by George. He was sitting in an aisle pew near the middle of the sanctuary. Mind you, we didn't know one another at the time. I'd only just met him that morning. He greeted me warmly, and I shook his hand. He spoke to me very kindly and with genuine appreciation for my earlier ministry that morning. He thanked me for my message and even commented on some of my points of emphasis.

I noticed he had his Bible on his lap, opened to the very passage I had preached on earlier. He then asked, "May I show you something?" Of course, I agreed. He directed my attention to 1 Samuel 3, just one chapter beyond my morning text. In the text, Samuel, still quite young, had been in the temple under Eli's teaching for about two years. George, with his wrinkled hand on his well-worn Bible, placed his index finger on a particular verse.

"Have you read this?" he asked. Chapter three recounts when God called young Samuel into His service; in the midst of

God's call, the biblical writer added this inspired insight: "Now *Samuel did not yet know the LORD*" (1 Samuel 3:7, emphasis mine). There it was, right in front of me, over the top of the old man's finger. It could not have been any plainer. I had just shouted from the rooftops that he had come to know Him at the age of three!

Admittedly, I was stunned. I must have looked like a deer caught in the headlights. I simply couldn't believe it. How had I missed that? (Hint: by not reading the context of my chosen passage.) What was I to do now? I wish I could tell you I was instantly convicted and realized my mistake (I did) and immediately acknowledged my error (I did not) and that as a first act in the pulpit that night I corrected my morning comments (I wish). No. Instead I babbled something about the possibility of it referring to Samuel not yet knowing the Lord in a deep way or some such silly thing.

> I THINK THAT ONE OF THE PROBLEMS WITH UNFETTERED ZEAL IS THAT, WHEN YOU'RE WRONG, IT'S TWICE AS HUMBLING TO GET HUMBLE.

Old George had been around the block a few times. He never brought it up again, and, while I'm sure he didn't buy my exegetical gymnastics, he hung in there with me as I became his pastor for the next twelve years.

I think that one of the problems with unfettered zeal is that, when you're wrong, it's twice as humbling to get humble. Yet that's exactly what we must do. As I've grown in my walk with Jesus, I've discovered that I'm still reluctant to acknowledge my wrong. My internal lawyer still rises up to my defense. I still wrestle with pride, as I did in my youth.

But I have learned the joy of genuine confession. When I pay attention to the promptings of the Holy Spirit, I am led to quicker confession.

EATING CROW

A few years back I made what some would consider an inappropriate comment from the pulpit. Truthfully, I quenched the Holy Spirit's prompting as I came to the prepared comment in my notes. I knew it would be provocative, but I had convinced myself (apparently because I had been listening only to myself!) that it would drive my point home in an unforgettable and effective way. I was right about the unforgettable part. Many folks enjoyed the provocative statement and even praised it. However, a number of people I admired and respected did not take so kindly to my words and rather gently let me know of their disappointment.

WE'VE ALL HEARD OF EATING CROW, AND WE ALL KNOW WHAT IT MEANS. BUT EATING IT WHEN IT'S YOUNG AND TENDER TOOK ON A WHOLE NEW MEANING FOR ME.

Thankfully, I was ready this time, and their rebuke hit the mark. My heart was convicted: I had sinned. And though my inner lawyer spoke up, as it always does, I knew I must plead guilty. I wrote an email to the church family confessing my wrong and asking their forgiveness. They were more than willing to release me of my debt. One response I received came from an older man, a recent convert. While new in the faith, he had been around the block a few times himself. He replied by saying that he forgave me, though he himself had not been offended by the comment. (On a side note, supportive comments like this may actually keep us from acknowledging our sins.) He went on to write this: "Pat, I really appreciated you humbling yourself on this matter. I have learned that the best time to eat crow is when it's young and tender." I still remember reading his statement and laughing out loud because it struck me as funny. We've all heard of eating crow, and we all know what it means. But eating it when it's *young and tender* took on a whole new meaning for me. It also encouraged me to work hard at identifying and confessing my sins as quickly as possible.

DOES IT LAND?

Sometimes we aren't sure whether we are wrong. In the book of Proverbs, there is a strange but powerful word picture that tells us how we can know if we are guilty of a sin and need to confess and forsake it quickly. Here it is: "Like a sparrow in its flitting, like a swallow in its flying, a curse that it causeless does not alight" (Proverbs 26:2).

Let me interpret that verse based on an experience I had at a church camp. Our men had just arrived at a beautiful, wooded camp bordering a lake. As we brought our gear into the cabin, a swallow flew into our room. I'm glad no one was filming, because these buff guys all reacted like little girls, minus the screaming. While the swallow darted back and forth, we all kept ducking up and down, *but it never landed on any of us.* The threat seemed real, but eventually the little bird found his way out the door and we collectively relaxed.

So it is with false curses or accusations against us. They don't land. They don't stick. They don't cause any conviction because they are not true. I try to judge the validity of an accusation against me by whether I feel convicted by the accusation itself.

C. S. Lewis wrote:

Surely what a man does when he is taken off his guard is the best evidence for what sort of a man he is. Surely what pops out before the man has time to put on a disguise is the truth. If there are rats in a cellar you are most likely to see them if you go in very suddenly. But the suddenness does not create the rats: it only prevents them from hiding. In the same way the suddenness of the provocation does not make me an ill-tempered man; it only shows me what an ill-tempered man I am. The rats are always there in the cellar, but if you go in shouting on noisily, they will have taken cover before you switch on the light.[5]

CULTIVATING HUMILITY

Someone has said that you can be wrong on your opinions but never on your facts. If you're wrong, as soon as this becomes clear by the conviction of the Holy Spirit, own your wrong.

One of the hardest things you can do is admit you're wrong, ... and one of the greatest things you can do is admit you're wrong. So, when was the last time you openly and humbly did so?

Learn to judge yourself not only by the facts but by your feelings in the moment.

Remember the flitting sparrow or the flying swallow. Did they land?

God's people are far more forgiving than we tend to believe. If you're wondering whether that's true, think of a time when someone—anyone—was genuinely humble over their wrong. Did you hesitate to forgive them? Probably not. There is something absolutely magnetic about humility. It is almost irresistible.

Keep short accounts with God, but keep them short with people, too. The crow will go down a lot easier for you.

SCRIPTURES FOR MEDITATION

Psalm 141:5; Proverbs 27:17

CHAPTER 3

DAVE LEONARD—
THE MAN WHO GAVE ME CLARITY

"If ya ain't who ya is, you'll be who ya ain't."

Titling a whole chapter after a man I barely knew may seem strange, but without his knowing it, Dave Leonard had an enormous impact on my Christian life and ministry.

A year and a half after I became a Christian, we sold our home in Waterloo, Iowa, and drove our half-filled U-Haul two hours southwest to Ankeny, Iowa, so I could attend Faith Baptist Bible College and pursue a pastoral degree.

The move meant not only relocating but reestablishing ourselves in a new church. Easier said than done. We left a church on fire for the gospel, with folks coming to Jesus regularly, then came to Saylorville Baptist Church, where they were not exactly blazing any trails in evangelism.

Our first church had moved at a frenetic pace in comparison to this one. Ironically, Saylorville is the church I currently pastor and have led for over twenty years but at that time focused more on education and biblical counseling. They were not seeing people saved with any regularity. Their pastor, a godly man with a tremendous understanding of Scripture and a determination to teach, taught verse-by-verse through the Bible. Even with solid teaching, the church people demonstrated little evidence of evangelistic zeal, and the baptismal waters remained relatively still.

Truthfully, we chose to join Saylorville with the hope that I might be able to bring an evangelistic dynamic to this body of believers while attending the nearby Bible college. As I soon discovered, however, *that* particular dynamic needs to come from the top down. Nevertheless, our pastor, though not strong on evangelism, did become a genuine friend and mentor to me. As a spiritually gifted man and teacher, he was God's man for me for that time in my life. He pointed me repeatedly back to the Word to find the answers for the questions I asked. In fact, he helped me long into my first pastorate through numerous phone conversations.

God appointed more than one person at that church to mentor and teach me. He had a number of very special people there who would deeply bless, impress, and direct my life during my college years. One of them was Dave Leonard.

Dave, already in his upper seventies when we met, had a son who served as a missionary to Brazil and grandsons who planned to follow in their dad's footsteps. Saylorville commissioned and sent out one of the grandsons for missionary service, and the church I later pastored in northern Iowa contributed to missionary support for the other one.

Dave's great-grandson Jerrod currently serves on the pastoral team at Saylorville Church. What a legacy! And it all started with Dave, who served as neither pastor nor missionary. He lived his life as what you might call a stateside missionary. He presented himself as a tough, rough, gruff, direct man, passionate for God and utterly intolerant of lazy Christianity. Clearly not your touchy-feely type. Few people went to Dave just to chat, but if you felt the need for a good kick in the pants, Dave was your man (there were few takers). Within two years, I had three encounters with him, each one powerful in and of itself. Each encounter also brought more clarity: clarity in terms of my vision of God, the message of God, and my calling from God. The last one came as a phone call that would eventually lead me to a retraction.

CLARITY IN MY VISION OF GOD

My very first encounter with Dave Leonard came at a midweek prayer meeting. The special open-microphone service gave folks the opportunity to publicly share whatever the Lord was doing in their lives. Dave and his little wife sat in the same place for every service: the front, left side of the main aisle, second row of pews. Pity the visitor who inadvertently sat there first, ignorant of who "owned" that spot! On this particular night, Dave rose first and took the microphone in his shaky hand. He stood, slightly bent over, with his back to the rest of us. His voice matched his disposition—rough—but there was a certain reverence in the atmosphere of the sanctuary as Dave, with Bible in hand, began to read. He opened to Isaiah 6. As he began reading the following words, a holy hush came over the congregation and over me:

> In the year that King Uzziah died I saw the Lord sitting upon a throne, high and lifted up; and the train of his robe filled the temple. Above him stood the seraphim. Each had six wings: with two he covered his face, and

with two he covered his feet, and with two he flew. And one called to another and said:

"Holy, holy, holy is the LORD of hosts;
the whole earth is full of his glory!" (Isaiah 6:1–3)

Then, closing his Bible, the bent-over saint slowly—very, very slowly—turned to the rest of us sitting behind him. With his wrinkled face, he stared at the congregation for no more than three seconds—though it seemed a full minute, at least. Then he asked, "How do you see Him?" before slowly turning back around and sitting down.

Whatever happened after that is a blur to me. But what was no longer a blur was my vision of God. The old man, by the simple, reverent reading of Scripture, had given me sight! A vision of a high and holy God. Every time I have read that passage since then, I think of Dave and that holy moment, now frozen in time to me, when I saw God as never before. From that moment on, I committed myself to seeing God more clearly and helping others to do the same.

CLARITY IN MY MESSAGE FROM GOD

The second encounter with Dave occurred outside a grocery store in our community. I was going in as he was coming out. He stopped me in my tracks and told me he had something he wanted to tell me. Now, when Dave Leonard talked, you listened because he did not make small talk. He believed in pouring truth, wisdom, or exhortation on his heart at that moment into his listeners, not caring whether or not the listener replied.

What's more, when Dave talked, he didn't look at you until he felt the need. He always looked away as he talked, but he expected you to be looking at him! Time and age had diminished his frame from a youthful 6'2" or 6'3", but I'm only 5'8", so I looked up to Dave whether or not he looked at me.

One comment in the middle of Dave's story that day literally became a "true north" in my life. He said, "Pat, I've been thinking about you, and I want you to pay attention to me. It's about preaching the gospel to lost people. I was down at the mission one day, preaching the gospel . . ." Until that moment he lectured as usual, while looking away. Then, as though in slow motion (the same way he had turned around in church after reading Isaiah), he pivoted and looked directly at me, maybe six inches from my face. With his piercing eyes leveled at me, he commented parenthetically, "You don't dare preach anything else at a mission," before going on with his story.

Whatever he said after that is a blur to me. He had literally tattooed me with the statement "You don't dare preach anything else at a mission." Instantly, I thought, "Of course! Lost people don't need to hear about how to be better husbands and wives and employees and citizens. They need the gospel!"

Dave had no more idea of how he impacted the formation of my life with that statement than when he had quoted from Isaiah 6. At that moment I determined I would never again have a conversation with another non-follower of Jesus without keeping their eternal destiny in my view. Once again, God used Dave Leonard to give me clarity—clarity in terms of my message from God.

As far as I can recall, in my 35 years of preaching there has never been a Sunday morning in either of the two churches I have pastored when the gospel was not preached or salvation offered to those in attendance. Sadly, on numerous occasions when guest speakers have finished speaking, I have had to supplement their message with a brief gospel invitation. Recently, a faithful family in our church who had moved here from another state shared how they had whittled down their search for a new church to two candidates: ours and one other. The wife remarked, "We liked both churches very much, but when it came to inviting our nonbelieving neighbors, we instantly knew Saylorville was the church for us." By the way, those nonbelieving neighbors are now faithful followers of Jesus and even serve in our church today. I owe so much of my evangelistic philosophy to Dave Leonard.

As you have seen, Dave behaved like a modern-day prophet in my life. But this book is about retractions. My third encounter with him led to a retraction in my life—one that did not come until years later—and it all took place on the phone.

CLARITY IN MY CALLING FROM GOD

As I have said, we attended a biblically solid church during my college days, but one that for years had not seen many people come to Christ. The pastor, though a good friend, outstanding counselor, and excellent Bible teacher, was not dynamic. In addition, he could be rather lengthy and sometimes monotone, which made focusing a challenge for a student working the graveyard shift—me.

I worked for UPS from 11:00 p.m. to 3:00 a.m. on weekdays during my college years, usually getting to bed by 4:00 a.m. If I could fall asleep, I'd get about three hours of shut-eye before heading off to school; then to study; then back to the family; and, finally, off again to work. Over time, this took its toll on me, especially on Sunday mornings while sitting in a warm church on a cushioned seat during a long message delivered in something of a monotone. I still remember nodding off one time, my wife gently elbowing me in my side—except that I didn't react as though it were a gentle elbow. I lurched straight up as though someone had electrocuted me. Everyone in the four rows around me got a chuckle. I didn't often let my attention drift or fall asleep in church, but when I did, let's just say I made it memorable.

Speaking of attention, early in our time at Saylorville the pastor attended a college Sunday School class I taught. My passion caught his attention, and not long afterward he invited me to speak on a Sunday morning. I felt absolutely giddy with excitement. I had preached in several smaller venues, but this was a church of three hundred people. I could hardly wait for this incredible opportunity to "cut loose" in the pulpit. When the day came, I came out preachin'! What I lacked in depth I made up for in zeal.

As it turned out, the Lord would bless me in the proclamation of His Word that day. God's people encouraged and affirmed this young whippersnapper. The contrasting style of high energy I brought to the pulpit apparently awakened a few other sleeping saints. As I recall, a young woman even walked the aisle to declare her trust in Christ. As a result, I almost floated home on a cloud of joy.

That's when my cloud burst. As we walked into our little apartment, the phone rang. It was Dave Leonard. The conversation went almost exactly like this:

"Hello, Nemmers."

"Pat, Dave Leonard here."

"Oh, hi Dave."

"Good message today." (Dave rarely gave out compliments, so, that one felt really good.)

"Thanks, brother."

"The reason I'm calling is to tell you something you need to hear."

"Okay." (I swallowed hard.)

"Nemmers, remember this—you're a preacher, not a teacher."

(I was stymied.)

"Ah. Yeah. Thanks. But I'm also a teacher and a Bible expositor." (Bear in mind that I was a theological student at the time, and we all wanted to become outstanding expositional Bible preachers. Being called simply a preacher had a kind of shallow ring to it. My pride was kicking in.)

Dave doubled down: "Listen, Nemmers, we've got enough teachers and counselors standing in our pulpits. We need preachers! Men who preach to lost souls. That's what you are, Nemmers: a preacher, not a teacher. That's all I've got to say."

And he hung up.

I experienced a major letdown. In fact, his comments ticked me off. Why couldn't he have left well enough alone, concluding with "Good message today"? Or, better yet, have shared with me all the great thoughts in my message that had moved him. Or recounted how I had preached to *his* soul? At least he could have waited a day or two before pulling me back down to earth.

But God had wired Dave Leonard as an exhorter: one who sees a need, observes and assesses a situation or individual, and addresses it or them directly (and apparently as soon as possible). That's what exhorters do. Dave saw in me a gift for preaching. He also saw before him a veritable landscape of preachers who did not passionately proclaim the gospel.

Sadly, at the time I heard his words as insults, but they were meant to *direct* me and *clarify* my calling from God. Unfortunately, my pride became my inhibitor. It took years for me to both see and accept the truth Dave spoke to me that day. Truth often acts like a time-release capsule; its medicine is dispensed over time. That's the area in which I could most glorify God, and that's what I would pursue.

Interestingly, I had been given that same lesson by another exhorter shortly before this. While powerful, however, the encounter had not been personal, and *that* ultimately made the difference. I had attended a Back to the Bible conference in Omaha, Nebraska. At the time, Back to the Bible reached a worldwide audience through their large radio ministry,

> TRUTH OFTEN ACTS LIKE A TIME-RELEASE CAPSULE; ITS MEDICINE IS DISPENSED OVER TIME.

led by Warren Wiersbe, a prolific author, pastor, and radio speaker. Chuck Swindoll, a well-known pastor, author, and radio speaker himself, was the keynote speaker for the conference that year. All the young, aspiring preachers followed him in those days.

Warren interviewed Chuck just before his message, asking him, "Chuck, what's the best advice you can give to the many young preachers in our audience?" I had secured a seat just off the platform, hoping to catch an audience with either Wiersbe or Swindoll after the service. Hearing Warren's question to Chuck, I leaned forward in anticipation of his answer. Clearly, Swindoll was not anticipating the spontaneous Q & A. He hesitated a bit, possibly because he had not yet preached his keynote message that evening. "The best advice? Hmm . . . The best advice I can give to you young guys pursuing ministry is to be who God made you to be."

Suddenly, Swindoll seemed to experience a fresh infilling of the Spirit, as his tongue freed up and all hesitation melted

> IT'S ALWAYS HUMBLING TO REALIZE THAT YOU HAVEN'T BEEN VIEWING A SITUATION AS CLEARLY AS YOU SHOULD HAVE BEEN. IT'S EVEN MORE HUMBLING WHEN THAT "SITUATION" IS YOU.

away. "I spent the first several years of ministry trying to copy all the popular preachers of the fifties and sixties." He actually started naming them. "Frankly, that was frustrating and exhausting. *The greatest day of my ministry life was the day I learned to be myself.* So, I'd say, you men should listen to the advice of the old country bumpkin who said, 'You gots to be who ya is, cause if ya ain't who ya is, you'll be who ya ain't.' So, by all means, be who ya is."

The place roared in laughter. I thought it funny, too, but mostly I thought it powerful.

Powerful advice, that is. I needed it then, and I need it now.

Powerful but not personal. In fact, I kept right on trying to imitate the great preachers of the eighties and nineties—Briscoe, MacArthur, Rogers, and—yes—Swindoll!

That's when Dave called . . .

CULTIVATING HUMILITY

It's always humbling to realize that you haven't been viewing a situation as clearly as you should have been. It's even more humbling when that "situation" is *you*. We often don't see ourselves as clearly as we think we do. I learned that the hard way. I once pulled together my entire pastoral team, along with a few ministry directors, and asked them to speak plainly (without fear of resistance from me) on what they saw in me that they wished I would change. *There were a lot of things in me they wanted to see changed!*

Argh. But I had asked for it.

Praise the Lord, the result was that I began to see myself more clearly.

I suspect that all of us have Dave Leonards who come into our lives. The question is, Will we see them as God's gifts for better focus and clarity or just as grumpy annoyances to ignore? Dave, it turned out, was a gift of clarity to me. He wasn't insulting me but *directing* me in the clarity of my calling. Years later, I still preach and teach and work diligently with the biblical text. But now I do so knowing not only my own gifts but my limitations as well. "What do you have that you did not receive?" (1 Corinthians 4:7)

Clarity Questions

If I were to ask you what your calling in life is and then ask someone close to you what they think about your calling in life, would the answers be the same? Is there someone who has spoken a hard word to you that you originally resented but now recognize as direction rather than an insult? Did it help bring clarity to your life's purpose? If so, have you thanked them?

Thank God for the Dave Leonards He brings or has brought into your life. He might be using them to direct your calling and help you to see more clearly.

SCRIPTURES FOR MEDITATION

John 21:22; 1 Corinthians 4:7; 1 Peter 4:10–11

CHAPTER 4

THE LURE OF LEGALISM

"Stick with the Bible's sins, Pastor.
There's plenty of them you can preach."

When I think about the first church I pastored, I am so thankful for those godly saints who loved the Lord and knew their Bibles. God used many of them to help me recant and repent of unbiblical areas of my life and ministry. One of these individuals was Bill Clark. One Sunday I joked from the pulpit, directing the congregation to "open your Bibles to one of the clean pages" as I led them to an obscure chapter in the book of Ezekiel. By "clean pages," I meant ones that were both unmarked and, for many, unread. At the end of my sermon, Bill and another older saint presented me with their "clean pages"—full of personal notes from years of study!

Point taken.

Back then, I was zealous about all things spiritual but not always biblical. I loved the Bible and prided myself on preaching it accurately and fervently, but I also took extrabiblical positions on dress; movies; marriage; divorce; alcohol; who did and didn't baptize; and yes, music. The steady stream of people coming to know Jesus, being baptized (by me, of course), and filling up the church felt wonderful, exciting, and glorious. Those results may have been the reason several of God's people chose to turn a blind eye to my extrabiblical excesses. I began gathering a legalistic army of faithful, well-intentioned followers who not only followed Jesus but also followed *me*! Looking back, the problem was that I'm not sure how carefully I was following Jesus or His Word on a number of those extrabiblical topics.

Those bothered by my excesses were smaller in number, and they generally kept their misgivings to themselves because they truly loved what God was doing and loved me. I loved them, too, but I'm sad to recall that I mentally inserted an asterisk next to their names. After all, they were spiritually weaker—or so I thought. My strong personality added another layer to my legalistic armor, making it even harder for them to get through to me. One member of this minority was Bill. Finally, there came a Sunday when he could no longer take it. One of my extrabiblical rants led to an uncharacteristic reaction from him, and the incident paved the way to my next retraction.

I honestly don't remember what I'd preached that day, but I clearly got wound up over one of those extrabiblical issues. Affirmed by an occasional "Amen!" from my larger army, I closed the service and stood by the door shaking hands as one admirer after another passed by, giving me the expected "'atta boy." Finally, Bill walked up.

As one of the godly older saints mentioned earlier, Bill had always worked hard, lived modestly, and raised his family "in the discipline and instruction of the Lord" (Ephesians 6:4).

People knew him for his love of the Bible and his winsome ability to teach it. Though not a confrontational man, he spoke with honesty and realism. Two years earlier, the church had not had a pastor, the membership numbers had been down in the thirties, and most of the members had been in their fifties, sixties, and seventies. Bill had stood up during the midweek prayer service and stated the obvious: "Folks, we need to face the reality that we're dying. We're a dying church. If God doesn't intervene, we'll soon have to close these doors."

Somebody had to say it. Everybody was thinking it, so Bill said it, and they proceeded to pray. As God would have it, that very weekend a young couple with their new baby walked into church. They were the first visitors to this little congregation in years. Nick (whom I mentioned in chapter 2) and Sandy, both of whom I had led to Christ, had just moved up to the area and were looking for a church. They were an answer to the dying church's prayer and, unknowingly, the precursor to my becoming their pastor. This was all because Bill had the guts to say the obvious and to call the church to prayer.

So, when I preached my heart out that more recent Sunday morning, not just from the Bible but beyond it, Bill just had to speak. As I said, most of the folks in our now-larger church passed by, shook my hand, and affirmed my strong message. I took Bill's hand to shake it but immediately perceived an unfamiliar sternness about him. Bill loved good Bible preaching and was one of my greatest encouragers. But not that day. I will never forget his powerful and direct words: "Stick with the Bible's sins, Pastor. There's plenty of them you can preach."

Immediately, I began to defend my words from my message, but I could tell my defensive stance only brought heartache to

Bill. He said nothing except to repeat his exhortation: "Stick with the Bible's sins." And he walked on.

At that moment, I was upset. There had been so much Bible truth in that sermon to which he could have alluded. Why did he have to focus on the stuff I had said that went beyond the Scripture? The answer was simple, and I've already stated it—Bill was a Bible guy, and that's what I loved about him. That's what I aspired to be, . . . and that's what I still needed to become.

Bill's rebuke hurt me, but it also helped me. I could not shake his words from echoing in my mind. "Stick with the Bible's sins, Pastor. There's plenty of them you can preach."

> JUST BECAUSE YOU ARE STRONG ON A CERTAIN ISSUE DOESN'T MAKE YOU BIBLICAL. IT JUST MAKES YOU STRONG.

Eventually those words would lead me to another retraction: stop placing personal standards on the same level as Scripture.

A few years later, having retracted my position on one of the extrabiblical subjects mentioned, I said this while teaching: "Just because you are strong on a certain issue doesn't make you biblical. It just makes you strong." The strong, authoritative people out there, despite their ability to influence others, do not prove they are right on a given subject simply by combining strong words with human reasoning. There is a pejorative term for those kinds of people: *demagogues*. God Himself has strong words for those of us who go beyond His Word: "Do not add to his words, lest he rebuke you and you be found a liar" (Proverbs 30:6).

Then there's Jesus's rebuke of the legalists of His day: "You hypocrites! Well did Isaiah prophesy of you, when he said: 'This people honors me with their lips, but their heart is far from me; in vain do they worship me, teaching as doctrines the commandments of men'" (Matthew 15:7–9).

Then there's Paul: "I have applied all these things to myself and Apollos for your benefit, brothers, that you may learn by us not to go beyond what is written, that none of you may be puffed up in favor of one against another" (1 Corinthians 4:6). Adding to Scripture, distorting Scripture, or going beyond Scripture are all strongly condemned *by* Scripture!

One of my favorite extrabiblical statements on legalism comes from John MacArthur: "A human standard might be more lenient than Scripture or more restrictive than Scripture, but it can never be better than Scripture."

Boom!

Human nature struggles to let God be God or let the Bible say what the Bible says. Human nature loves to go beyond the Word of God. While priding myself on being a "Bible guy," I became what author Larry Osborne calls an accidental Pharisee. I unintentionally added human reasoning to several things God had already addressed in Scripture . . . and only as clearly as He saw fit.

The Pharisees are the case study in legalism from the New Testament. Their name means "separated ones," and their stance became synonymous with legalism. Osborne, in his excellent book *Accidental Pharisees*, takes us from the old-school legalism of yesterday to the new-school legalism of today. Old-school legalism wondered *What's in your refrigerator?* concerned that you might be harboring beer or wine. The new school wonders *What's in your driveway?* referring to the status symbol you may possess in the vehicle you drive. But it's all the same. Legalism has been defined in various ways but can be summarized as attempting to gain spiritual acceptance before God by outward conformity to the man-made rules of the day.

For example, I was the evening speaker for a week at a Christian camp. In the middle of the week, my wife and I did a Q & A with the campers, who were mostly adults and high schoolers. The campers submitted their questions in advance to the moderator, and one of them asked about my position on alcohol. Now, this particular camp in large part represented churches with long histories of taking very strong (and sometimes extrabiblical) positions on drinking. I knew that. In fact, I had for a very long time held the same position. I wanted to be respectful of my audience, but I also wanted to be truthful. I kept my answer short but made clear that the Bible calls drunkenness (the giving up of one's self-control) a sin but does not make the same claim for the consumption of alcohol per se. I also took the time to address my personal concerns regarding those who sin by flaunting their personal liberty with regard to alcohol consumption in front of those who might not consider themselves to have the same liberty (read Romans 14). I knew I was on a tightrope with the nearly four hundred attendees, but the feedback I received encouraged me that I had not stepped off the rope. I believed I had handled the subject rightly and with respect. Then I received a letter . . .

This personal, typewritten letter (from an actual typewriter) excoriated me for taking advantage of a Baptist camp representing mostly Baptist churches that took a stance against any consumption of alcohol. It was not a letter requesting dialogue on the subject but a full-on assault against my position, while making much of the history of the churches represented in the camp. The writer's attempt to validate his position using verses from the Bible suggested that he had taken his cues from someone else some time back. I never responded to the gentleman. I'm fairly certain he wasn't looking for a response.

Jesus saved His harshest language for the pharisaical legalists of his day. I know the following is lengthy, but it's worth reading. I can assure you that Jesus does not waste one word:

> The scribes and the Pharisees sit on Moses' seat, so do and observe whatever they tell you, but not the works they do. For they preach, but do not practice. They tie up heavy burdens, hard to bear, and lay them on people's shoulders, but they themselves are not willing to move them with their finger. They do all their deeds to be seen by others. For they make their phylacteries broad and their fringes long, and they love the place of honor at feasts and the best seats in the synagogues and greetings in the marketplaces and being called rabbi by others. But you are not to be called rabbi, for you have one teacher, and you are all brothers. And call no man your father on earth, for you have one Father, who is in heaven. Neither be called instructors, for you have one instructor, the Christ. The greatest among you shall be your servant. Whoever exalts himself will be humbled, and whoever humbles himself will be exalted.
>
> But woe to you, scribes and Pharisees, hypocrites! For you shut the kingdom of heaven in people's faces. For you neither enter yourselves nor allow those who would enter to go in. Woe to you, scribes and Pharisees, hypocrites! For you travel across sea and land to make a single proselyte, and when he becomes

a proselyte, you make him twice as much a child of hell as yourselves.

Woe to you, blind guides, who say, "If anyone swears by the temple, it is nothing, but if anyone swears by the gold of the temple, he is bound by his oath." You blind fools! For which is greater, the gold or the temple that has made the gold sacred? And you say, "If anyone swears by the altar, it is nothing, but if anyone swears by the gift that is on the altar, he is bound by his oath." You blind men! For which is greater, the gift or the altar that makes the gift sacred? So whoever swears by the altar swears by it and by everything on it. And whoever swears by the temple swears by it and by him who dwells in it. And whoever swears by heaven swears by the throne of God and by him who sits upon it.

Woe to you, scribes and Pharisees, hypocrites! For you tithe mint and dill and cumin and have neglected the weightier matters of the law: justice and mercy and faithfulness. These you ought to have done, without neglecting the others. You blind guides, straining out a gnat and swallowing a camel!

Woe to you, scribes and Pharisees, hypocrites! For you clean the outside of the cup and the plate, but inside they are full of greed and self-indulgence. You blind Pharisee! First clean the inside of the cup and the plate, that the outside also may be clean.

Woe to you, scribes and Pharisees, hypocrites! For you are like whitewashed tombs, which outwardly appear beautiful, but within are full of dead people's bones and all uncleanness. So you also outwardly appear righteous to others, but within you are full of hypocrisy and lawlessness.

Woe to you, scribes and Pharisees, hypocrites! For you build the tombs of the prophets and decorate the monuments of the righteous, saying, "If we had lived in the days of our fathers, we would not have taken part with them in shedding the blood of the prophets." Thus you witness against yourselves that you are sons of those who murdered the prophets. Fill up, then, the measure of your fathers. You serpents, you brood of vipers, how are you to escape being sentenced to hell? Therefore, I send you prophets and wise men and scribes, some of whom you will kill and crucify, and some you will flog in your synagogues and persecute from town to town, so that on you may come all the righteous blood shed on earth, from the blood of righteous Abel to the blood of Zechariah the son of Barachiah, whom you murdered between the sanctuary and the altar. Truly, I say to you, all these things will come upon this generation. (Matthew 23:2–36).

Why have I included Jesus's lengthy denunciation of the Pharisees in this book? Because to retract and repent of legalism is no small thing. It is to see the lure of legalism as nothing less than wickedness. Allow me to repeat some of Jesus's choice phrases from the passage above: "Woe to you . . . hypocrites! . . . you shut the kingdom of heaven in people's faces . . . You make [others] child[ren] of hell." In other words, your hypocrisy keeps people out of heaven! But Jesus did not stop with His denunciations:

"Fools! . . . Blind! . . . full of greed and self-indulgence . . . whitewashed tombs! . . . You also outwardly appear righteous

to others, but within you are full of hypocrisy and lawlessness
. . . You serpents, you brood of vipers, how are you to escape
being sentenced to hell?" These are not merely words of
denunciation; they are words of *damnation!* For Christ's sake,
don't take them lightly.

Today, I still preach the Bible expositionally, and I still preach
on sin. Many sins. What do ya know? There really are plenty of them
to choose from, and they come with some stiff warnings attached!
I discovered to my surprise that some of the things I had once
preached so passionately against are not referred to in Scripture as
sinful. In most cases, such practices require discernment, leaving
the true Christ-follower with the work of determining before
God the right course of action in a given situation. Many times
our choice—because of its possible influence on a weaker brother
or sister—will necessitate refraining from some liberty. At other
times we will be free, by faith, to partake in our liberty (Romans
14:22). Wisdom will take in both our dedication to the Lord and
our love for our fellow brother or sister.

Bill was right, of course. He went to heaven before I had a
chance to retract my defense of my extrabiblical positions. I look
forward to the day we meet again. He will then be able to say to
me, "See, I told you so!" But, knowing Bill, he'll probably just hug
me and rejoice in the grace of God that both saves and sanctifies.
On that day, there will be no more sins to preach on! Hallelujah!

CULTIVATING HUMILITY

It is a good thing for us to remind ourselves that adding to God's
Word is a temptation intrinsic to our sinful nature. The lure of
legalism is powerful. Take an inventory of the issues you are

passionate about. Are they biblical? Do they belong in the category of foundational theological truth? Or is your passion about a preference not addressed specifically in the Bible? If so, the issue is not something you should press upon others.

> IT IS A GOOD THING FOR US TO REMIND OURSELVES THAT ADDING TO GOD'S WORD IS A TEMPTATION INTRINSIC TO OUR SINFUL NATURE.

During his retirement years, the noted author, Warren Wiersbe, befriended Zach, a young theology student I later mentored. One day Dr. Wiersbe pulled out his personal notepad and wrote a kind warning on the lures of legalism to our mutual friend. Because he etched these words on the notepad, he delivered a concise message (I actually have a cherished photocopy of the note). Here are the words Wiersbe scratched out and sent Zach:

> Zach,
> There's a difference between
> convictions, opinions, and prejudices.
> With convictions we say "I know" and are
> willing to go to jail for it.
> With opinions, we say "I think" and are
> willing to consider other points of view.
> With prejudices, we say "I feel" and really
> don't have reasons why!
> W.W.W.

We hate to admit it, but our flesh loves extrabiblical additions. Beware the praise that comes not from biblical conviction but from personal preference.

The following are 14 signs I've collected over time (not all unique to me) that might identify you as a legalist:

Fourteen Signs That You Might Be Legalistic

1. You read your Bible to get a check mark rather than to meet with God.
2. Your spiritual disciplines define your spirituality.
3. You refuse to forgive although you've been forgiven.
4. You judge others before you listen to them.
5. You justify yourself by comparing yourself to others.
6. You feel the need to point out someone else's sin publicly.
7. Your schedule is so tight it doesn't have room for "If the Lord wills" in it.
8. You separate your spiritual life from your natural life.
9. You spend time only with "saved" people.
10. You love the praise of men more than the smile of God.
11. You're more interested in conformity than conversion.
12. You make little things big and big things little.
13. You praise only other's outward deeds.
14. You reject the truth tellers who come into your life.

Take some extra time to go over those 14 signs. Do any of them resonate with and convict you? Highlight them. Then get on your knees and acknowledge them to God for what they are: wickedness before Him. Seek His forgiveness and commit to retracting them from your life, once and for all.

SCRIPTURES FOR MEDITATION

1 Corinthians 4:6; Galatians 1:10

CHAPTER 5

A VALENTINE'S DAY CONFESSION

"I always take pains to have a clear conscience
toward both God and man."

ACTS 24:16

The Indian spiritual leader Dada Vaswani once said, "The best sleeping pill is a good conscience." I believe that's true, especially for a Christian who knows he is a child of the living God and sleeps under His care.

I will never forget the day after I first trusted in Jesus and committed myself to Him as His follower. I remember walking around the house, continuously thinking, *My sins are forgiven. My sins are all forgiven!*

That thought absolutely enthralled me because my life before Jesus had been an absolute mess, with an incredibly high stack of ongoing sins: lying, cheating, stealing, vulgarity, and addiction. Along with my two-packs-a-day cigarette addiction, I puffed on a lot of marijuana: every day, four to six times a day, I toked up. This state was my *normal*, so I literally smoked to get normal. I did other drugs, but I always preferred weed. After my epic crossover from spiritual death to life, darkness to light, and hell to heaven, my life radically changed. Within a few weeks God rescued me from both pot and cigarettes. My "factory" mouth went from four-letter words no one should say to ones that brought glory to God. Above it all, I loved, adored, worshipped, and spoke up for Jesus. Truly, "[The LORD] put a new song in my mouth, a song of praise to our God." In time, "many [would] see and fear, and put their trust in the LORD" (Psalm 40:3).

My radical conversion was soon followed by my wife, Nina's, less radical but no less amazing conversion to Christ. I've told our congregation multiple times, "You don't have to have an incredible story, but you do have to have a *credible* story." Nina's conversion was more than credible, and God accomplished a great, saving work in her life. Before long, we were both sharing our faith with family and friends while enjoying our new and growing spiritual family and group of friends.

YOU DON'T HAVE TO HAVE AN INCREDIBLE STORY, BUT YOU DO HAVE TO HAVE A CREDIBLE STORY.

My brother Mike, who had led me to Christ, soon began urging me to consider pursuing a theological education, as well as full-time ministry. I started receiving requests to give my personal testimony in different venues. Opportunities to share my story ranged from one-on-one conversations to high school, college, and church settings to speaking at my brother's little country church to even having a church planter give me preaching opportunities in little start-up churches. I constantly told my story.

My "come to Jesus" testimony never changed, but it did

expand. The more I spoke, the more I would remember one detail after another that showed the sharp contrast between who I had been and what God had done and was still doing in my life. One night, after returning from the church visitation program, I was telling my story to a small group of men, including David Graham, the pastor of our church. Pastor Graham, a tall, handsome Southern man, listened with great attention. When I finished, he said, "Pat Nemmers, I'd like you to share your testimony with the church this Sunday night." Beside myself with joy, I accepted! It would be my first time sharing my testimony publicly in *my* church. Even before I could soak in the thrill of the invitation, Pastor Graham added this: ". . . . and don't spare a detail."

I already loved sharing my story of God's grace, adding details as they came to mind, but one area of my past troubled me deeply. I never spoke of it, and I left it out that first night I testified in church.

Unsure of how to handle this troubling "detail," I shared it with my brother Mike during a golf game just weeks after my coming to trust Jesus. Mike didn't just play golf with me. He poured time and energy into my spiritual life. He regularly drove three hours one way just to disciple me, teaching spiritual and theological truths, including his own personalized version of the famous Walk Thru the Bible's demonstration of how the Old Testament unfolds.[6] This allowed me to connect threads of truth I had never even known existed in the Bible. I will forever be indebted to Mike for the time he invested in me during my first few years as a Christian.

Mike was not only my sibling but a trusted brother in Christ, and I wanted his guidance with this troubling area of my past: I had been unfaithful to my wife, Nina, both before and after we were married. As an unsaved, unmarried man, I had given in to sexual temptation a number of times. Adding shame upon shame, I had committed adultery after Nina and I were married. While I did not have an affair, it was still adultery. Even as a non-Christian, that break of trust had really bothered me—but not enough to confess it. Now, for me as a Christian, that past act of unfaithfulness bothered me on an even deeper level. And all of this was unknown to Nina, including the fact that I had been unfaithful to her before our marriage.

I needed help.

As I thought it over, I knew I'd been forgiven in salvation, but something told me that this wasn't enough. During the golf game, as Mike and I made our way down a fairway, I told him my story and shared the guilt I still carried.

"Should I tell Nina?" I asked.

My brother was not quick to answer. I can still picture him, head down and mind contemplating as we made our way to the green. I knew what he was thinking. Nina was a new believer, just a few weeks old in Christ. She was also right in the middle of her studies to become a registered nurse. Her conversion was real, but she had experienced so many new responsibilities and changes—not just the pressures of nursing school, but a new church, new friends, and a new way of life. Mike was deliberating all of this, and finally he broke his silence. "Pat, I wouldn't say anything to Nina. That knowledge could really devastate her right now. Your sins are forgiven. You don't have to bear that guilt any longer. I'd move on without telling her. The Lord knows."

Before you think my brother gave me bad advice, I believe he was right. Nina *was* very young in the faith. She *was* already overstretched with studies. There *was* wisdom in his words to wait.

So, I did. But not forever.

Over the next year I sensed the call of God to full-time ministry, and as we walked in obedience to God's direction we experienced a whirlwind of change. Within six months of my conversion, I was preaching in many different venues. I continued to share my ever-unfolding story, but in reviewing the litany of sins I had formerly committed, I simply mentioned that I had been an "immoral man." I gave no explanation, and usually the general comment went over everyone's head, including Nina's. But the word "immoral" only bandaged my damaged conscience, as I rationalized that I was not covering up—not entirely, anyway.

Nine years after our salvation and five years into our first pastorate, God continued to bless us. Our little family grew to four healthy children, and our little country church grew, too. Life was good. Church life was good. All was good—all, that is, except my conscience.

My past, pre-salvation sin still clawed at me.

During those nine years, I can truthfully say I never once lied to Nina or anyone else regarding my past infidelity. I did, however, find myself dancing around the edges of the truth on several occasions. Still, whenever I shared my testimony, I generally admitted to having been "immoral." Immorality encompasses a broad range, and I assuaged my conscience with the use of that word. Honestly, Nina never once asked what I meant by "immoral"—that is, until Valentine's Day 1991.

That evening, after our children were asleep, we enjoyed our Valentine's Day. We made love and then lay beside one another in bed and just talked. I can still see her face as she looked into my eyes with such love. Then she said something I never saw coming. "Isn't it wonderful we were both virgins when we got married?" I was completely taken off guard and stunned. And

Nina caught it in my eyes.

The moments that followed were the worst of my entire life. I had devastated her. Truthfully, even though the events had happened well over ten years earlier, hearing this was as painful to her as if I had committed those sins the night before. And my reasons for not telling her now sounded hollow.

Though devastated in her spirit, Nina heard my repentant, sorrowful confession and plea for forgiveness—now as a woman of deep faith.

The longest night of my life gave way to the coldest morning of our marriage. Then, to my surprise and soon delight, I came to the realization that the cold I had perceived was actually a time of deep, spiritual contemplation on Nina's part. The Holy Spirit led her to these words of Scripture: "Be kind to one another, tenderhearted, forgiving one another, as God in Christ forgave you" (Ephesians 4:32). Those words freed Nina to forgive me, once and for all: "If Jesus has forgiven me so much, how can I withhold forgiveness from you? I do forgive you." And she *did* forgive me. She never—and I mean *never*—brought it up again.

Don't misunderstand. She wept a lot. Sometimes, without warning, she cried, and I knew why. I always tried to comfort her, and though she never brushed me off, sometimes she just needed to cry. This went on for nearly two months, and she lost a considerable amount of weight. Clearly, she was in mourning, experiencing a kind of bereavement. Although forgiven, I felt the awful weight of what I had done to her.

Then, almost as quickly as the grief had weighed down Nina's spirit, it lifted. She became her old self again, and our ministry together, subdued during those months, also revived.

I went on sharing my testimony after that, but with a freedom of unexplainable confidence. Forgiveness freed my conscience, and a new boldness came with my repentance. I never shared any sordid details of my past sins. In fact, I felt more excited to talk about the grace of forgiveness given to and by Nina. What's more, my confessions never sent her spiraling backward. Because she was forgiven in Christ, she confidently forgave me, and I joyfully received her forgiveness. Nina lived just four and a half more years here on earth, and they were the best years of our marriage.

In my introduction, I wrote that retractions are all about taking an honest, humble look at your past sins, being willing to openly admit them, confess them, and repent of them. Then to keep confessing them, not only for your own benefit but for the benefit of others: they're about cultivating humility after being humbled. By continually confessing my already forgiven sins, I am aided in my pursuit of humility.

However, I did not yet realize that the next generation would need to learn of my failure and witness my confession.

Nearly ten years passed between the time I had first acknowledged my utter failure in marital fidelity and my confession to Nina, followed by her gracious forgiveness. Then, nearly 25 years later, I had to humbly confess the story all over again. The confession came not because of any further sin but because my own children were still unaware of how I had sinned against their mother.

I, like other public speakers, often share personal stories but tend to take certain things for granted. I somehow took for granted that my seven children knew all about my former indiscretions. Surely, they were aware of my life before Christ. In fact, my older ones were so familiar with my story that they once interrupted me as I shared my testimony with some visiting missionaries; they asked if they could tell the rest of it! I was both surprised and delighted to sit back and listen in on their version of my story. They knew it well and retold it clearly, . . . except the part about dad's infidelity. My oldest daughter had a vague understanding of my past sin, but the rest of my children did not know that part of the story any more than their mom had before my confession.

Fast forward 24 years after Nina's passing. My oldest son, who lives out east, visited us over Christmas in 2019. He, his younger brothers, and a friend planned to meet one afternoon at a sports bar to watch our favorite college football team on the big screen. I had not seen my son's friend in years, and, as we were catching up, the subject of spiritual things naturally flowed into the conversation. As I shared about the power of forgiveness, I explained how my first wife had forgiven me after I had committed adultery.

I didn't notice it then, but the information took my oldest son completely off guard, though he continued to sit quietly next to his friend. He later spoke to some of his siblings and soon discovered that they, too, were uninformed. When this finally got back to me, I was incredulous. *How could they not have known about this? I wondered. I have alluded to this at least half a dozen times from the pulpit.* Then it hit me. *Allude*: to refer to something indirectly.

I suddenly realized that I had never openly shared with my own, now adult children that part of the story Nina and I shared. How blind could I be? Very blind, it turned out.

My seven children were not only surprised to hear of my past sin against their mother, but some of them felt actual hurt—hurt that their dad would ever have done such a thing to their sweet mother, and hurt because I had alluded to the indiscretion *to the world* but had not specifically confessed it to them.

When my horrific oversight first dawned on me, I started making phone calls and having conversations with some of my kids. Then I thought, *No. They each need to hear the same story from me.* Even though most of my children lived within thirty minutes of our home, not all of them did, so I sat down and wrote the following confession and sent it to each of them:

Kids,

Knowing that the chances of getting all of us together to share these things is pretty remote, I thought I'd write to you.

During Christmas time, during a time I was with (one of their sibling's names here), I alluded to the love of your mother and the powerful example of forgiveness she demonstrated to me when I shared my past with her. Wrongly, I assumed that I had alluded to this enough that all of you already knew. I'm grateful to (another of their sibling's names here), who reminded me in a conversation that they themselves had only the vaguest recollection of the story. Of course, many, if not all, of you were too young for us, and later me, to tell the story. I'm profoundly sorry for this and for my presumptions. I ask you if you would please forgive me.

Briefly, here is the sad, yet beautiful story. Before salvation, I was unfaithful to your dear mother. She never knew. There are no excuses. No one—especially your beautiful mom—could have deserved such treachery as I was guilty of. That said, it was not an "affair" (horrible word) but a stupid, selfish, drunken, and sinful indiscretion. Though I was not yet saved, the guilt from the act haunted me even after salvation. Speaking of which, I confessed it to your uncle Mike shortly after my conversion. He counseled me not to tell your mom at that time (I'm not blaming Mike, just stating a fact) since she had just been saved herself and since God had already forgiven me. He was concerned that the truth would be too hard for her to take at the time.

I took his advice, albeit reluctantly, and went on with life. For the record, I never once lied to your mother (though one could argue that by not telling her I was lying). Then, on Valentine's Day, February 14, 1991, while we were lying next to one another, your beautiful mom looked tenderly into my eyes and said, "Isn't it wonderful we were both virgins when we got married?" (Forgive me again if this is more than you want to know.) I was completely taken off guard and stunned. And she caught it in my eyes.

The moments that followed were the worst of my entire life. I had devastated her. Truthfully, I might as well have committed the adulterous act the night before, though it had happened nearly ten years earlier. My explanation for not telling her before that time wasn't holding up well, either. But my sorrow, repentance, and plea for forgiveness (by the help of God) prevailed. After the hardest night of our lives and a cold early morning, your mother came to me. The very Scripture you kids had memorized in song (Ephesians 4:32) broke through to her heart. As I said, she came to me, still weeping. But through her tears, she pointed to the truth of God and said "How can I, after being forgiven so much by my Savior, withhold forgiveness from you? I do forgive you." With that, we wept together.

The next few months were hard. Really hard. Your mom cried—a lot. She lost a large amount of weight from involuntary fasting. She just didn't want to eat. We talked a lot. Made love a lot. And slowly, over time, the weeping subsided, her appetite returned, and our marriage was revived. Oh, and she got pregnant with Elizabeth. Elizabeth Joy, that is. God had brought joy back to our marriage.

Your amazing mother never—and I mean never—brought up my sin again. I realize few people are like her, but she never rubbed that truth in my face again. In fact, she even allowed me to share how she'd forgiven me whenever I would share my story, and she was fine with my doing so. The farther I get away from that time, the greater I stand amazed at the grace of God in her. The last five years of her life were truly the best of our marriage.

So, there it is. That's the story—as accurately as I can remember it. I hope it provides the knowledge you needed or wanted. And I pray the Lord may actually use it in your own lives and marriages.

Again, I am deeply sorry for not having thought of sharing this with you sooner. I ask each and all of you to forgive me for not doing so.

With great love for each of you,
Dad

There were a few more conversations, and I'm thankful that my children graciously forgave me. Humbly reviewing this past failure with my children made me pause and think: *surely God desires for me to not only preach the cultivation of humility after humiliation but to keep living it myself.*

CULTIVATING HUMILITY

I won't lie—this is going to be a hard one for some of you. Some of you have hidden issues in your past that need to be openly confessed, but you have not done it. And even if you don't have anything hidden, I believe there is a lesson on keeping short accounts found in the Old Testament.

In the book of Numbers, there is a principle that arrested me many years ago; I have applied it, however imperfectly, ever since. Listen to Moses's words:

> "If a woman vows a vow to the LORD and binds herself by a pledge, while within her father's house in her youth, and her father hears of her vow and of her pledge by which she has bound herself and says nothing to her, then all her vows shall stand, and every pledge by which she has bound herself shall stand. But if her father opposes her *on the day that he hears of it*, no vow of hers, no pledge by which she has bound herself shall stand. And the LORD will forgive her, because her father opposed her" (Numbers 30:3–5, emphasis mine).

In other words, there was a brief window of time during which the father of a daughter still under his authority could nullify his daughter's vow.

The principle I refer to is that we are to act quickly whenever God makes us aware of any situation in life requiring our immediate attention. This is especially true regarding the sins— big or small—we commit.

Not long ago, while I was exercising on an elliptical machine at our local gym, I was at the same time talking on my phone with a pastor friend who was seeking my advice on a certain matter. I wore my Air Pods, as did the people around me, so as not to disturb one another with our music or conversations. But let's just say that . . . my voice carries. A woman peddling a stationary bicycle a few feet from me looked up in frustration and signaled that I was being too loud. Not only did I not think I was too loud, but I rolled my eyes at her and even motioned with my hands as though to imply that she was overreacting.

The moment I gestured at her, my conscience convicted me, but it took about ten minutes for me to process my attitude and reaction. I knew I had sinned. As I finished up my workout, I confessed my sin to God and then humbly made my way over to where the woman was still peddling. I told her that my reaction had been both rude and wrong and asked her to please forgive me. She quickly did, and we ended with a pleasant conversation.

> I HAVE DISCOVERED OVER THE YEARS THAT THE SOONER I DEAL WITH MY SINS, THE MORE SENSITIVE I REMAIN TO THEM.

Obviously, I had not applied this principle earlier in my situation with Nina. But I have discovered over the years that the sooner I deal with my sins, the more sensitive I remain to them. By delaying my confession to my wife, I had not only prolonged my guilt but made things much harder on her when I finally admitted my sin. Thankfully, forgiveness may be granted here on earth from those who have received God's grace—like my family; even more importantly, forgiveness is always available from God (1 John 1:9).

SCRIPTURES FOR MEDITATION

Numbers 30; Psalm 66:18; Isaiah 59:1–2; 1 John 1:8–10

CHAPTER 6

STOP SELLING YOUR CHURCH!

"I am the Lord; that is my name; my glory I give to no other."
ISAIAH 42:8

O n my first Sunday in our country church, we had 27 people in attendance. The next Sunday we had only 21! *Is it too early to get discouraged?* I wondered. I called my brother, also a pastor in ministry for about five years, hoping for a sympathetic ear. Instead, he shot back, "Get back in there and preach like there are 2100!"

Ouch.

But that's exactly what I did. Within a year we had doubled in size, and within three years we averaged over eighty people. By then we had started a children's ministry, men's ministry, women's ministry, youth group, and choir. All along, folks were coming to Jesus, getting baptized, and joining the church. Our little church hummed along, and we loved being a part of it.

Among all our other programs, we started a "visitation" ministry from the very beginning. I'm not sure who came up with *visitation* as a name—we weren't going to funerals, after all, but visiting homes. We met with *living people*, humanly speaking, but in truth we visited *spiritually dead* people (see Ephesians 2:1–10). We talked with folks from the small towns around our church and occasionally to farmers in their farmhouses. We went out with a purpose—to share the gospel in a personal way with the hope of winning souls to new life in Jesus. The growth of our church came mainly through visiting people in their homes, with some unforgettable experiences along the way.

As the church progressed in terms of offering a program for nearly everyone, God Himself caught me undervaluing the message of the gospel, the very foundation of our church. This led me to a significant spiritual retraction. The realization came as I visited the home of a young, unmarried couple who were open to and very interested in our church. After visiting a bit and getting to know one another, I began telling them about our new young couples' ministry. Before I knew it, I'd moved on to talking about our energetic youth ministry. Looking at the couple, I then told them of our men's and women's ministries. I was on a roll. We really did have a lot going on! Then it happened. During my presentation—I mean, as I talked, looking right at the couple—the Holy Spirit spoke to my heart as clearly as He had ever spoken. He seemed to say, "Nemmers, what are you doing? When you first came to this church you had nothing—no program, no 'felt need' to draw folks in when you visited people. You had only Jesus. I liked that better. Why don't you get back to talking about Him?"

I remember being stunned in the moment—so stunned I nearly lost my train of thought. (And just as well. I was probably in the process of selling another program.) That powerful rebuke had come directly from the Holy Spirit, not after the fact but in the very midst of my selling the church and its wares instead of sharing about Jesus. It was as though God Himself observed (as He always does) and, fed up with my pitch, stopped me cold with "Enough!"

It was clear enough that, though the voice was not audible, I heard Him. I went from being stunned to being humbled. In midstream, while selling the church, I humbly refocused my presentation, centering the conversation on Jesus. That night, in that home, sharing with that couple in need of Christ, I repented of attempting to sell the church and made another retraction. With God's help—along with His occasional interruptions—I would never again sell the church to one whose greatest need was to enter the church through faith in Jesus.

> I WOULD NEVER AGAIN SELL THE CHURCH TO ONE WHOSE GREATEST NEED WAS TO ENTER THE CHURCH THROUGH FAITH IN JESUS.

DÉJÀ VU

Years later, I pastored a church that also "took off"—growing and expanding, adding more people, pastors, directors, and programs with all the bells and whistles. During those days, I discovered that I needed to learn the lesson of not "selling the church" all over again.

Nearly 15 years after my experience visiting the home of that young couple, I relearned this lesson in a different way. The Lord revealed to me that there were other ways of selling the church to outsiders that did not bring Him the honor He deserved. This humbling story is one I absolutely love telling because it not only put me in my place but blazed a trail for the ongoing cultivation of humility in my life and ministry.

WHEN BIGGER IS NOT ALWAYS BETTER

In the spring in 2004, my sixth year as pastor at Saylorville Church, I completed leading the church family through a major remodel and expansion. The changes took us out of the seventies, removing, among other things, the ubiquitous burnt orange carpet and matching pews that seemed to adorn so many churches in those days. We raised the money without borrowing, a philosophy I had introduced to our people early on. Because of this, a genuine feeling of accomplishment and a desire to walk by faith grew throughout the congregation.

But I wanted more. I wish I could say I wanted a God-honoring *kind* of more, but in reality, it was just more. I wanted bigger, not necessarily better.

With a congregation of five hundred (and growing), I thought the only thing missing was a gymnasium. Of course, I had all the unselfish reasons for having one: we could utilize it for children's and youth ministries, introduce sports outreaches, and enjoy big church and family events. I also loved the idea of afternoon basketball games with the staff for fun, exercise, and an opportunity for yearlong relief from the daily pressures of pastoral work. We already did some of that outside during the summer: we set up a basketball hoop in a flat area on the corner of our parking lot and even painted lines on the asphalt. We played out there when the weather permitted, . . . and sometimes when it didn't! For a few weeks one summer, we played in nearly one-hundred-degree temperatures, brutal on everything, but we loved it. Unfortunately, "weather permitting" implied that weather did not always permit playing outdoors. An indoor facility would allow us to play all the time. That sounds legit, doesn't it?

Almost immediately following the completion of the church expansion and remodel, with all my excellent reasons in hand, I proposed that we begin a capital campaign to raise money for a gymnasium.

It was a bad idea.

Our people were tapped out financially. They had just sacrificially given thousands of dollars without borrowing, and now I was asking them to do it again. I've had smarter days.

With a few more filters in my life, I might not have made such a wrongheaded proposal. I wasn't selling the church per se, but I was pitching a plan. As it turned out, it wasn't one the Lord was swinging at, and neither was our church.

In reality, God sovereignly used my miscalculation to bring about something better, not bigger. But I'm getting ahead of myself.

In my zeal for a gymnasium, we renewed our relationship with our architect; we had the drawings made up, and I pitched the new plan to the church membership. Our people did not "click their heels" over the plan, but we were committed, . . . or so I thought. Yet when we took up the special offering and tallied the total monies, the result was more like taking up an offering to help the junior boys go to camp, not the raising of money to build a gymnasium.

My dreams for a gym fell with a thud, leaving me heartsick and stunned, but I shouldn't have been surprised. The church sent their pastor a clear message: "We're tired, stretched, and maybe broke. Come back to us another time, please." I did swing back to the issue ten years later (a story for another time), but at that moment I had no idea when or if that day would come.

Our staff of three pastors sat around the small round conference table in my office the Monday morning after that pitiful offering. I felt so discouraged, with my hopes for a gymnasium dashed. What's more, at that moment I doubted my own ability as a leader, with such little evidence of the church following my lead on this project. I recognized my poor timing and lack of wisdom in this situation and understood that no more money would be raised based on the dreams of so few.

As the harsh reality settled in to the three of us, Kevin Thomas, our counseling pastor at the time, unexpectedly and almost under his breath, remarked, "Maybe it's time we plant a church." His quiet words brought on my epiphany.

"What did you say?" I asked.

Kevin, not a man easily given to emotion, always thought before speaking, and this time was no exception. He repeated himself: "Maybe we should plant a church. I mean, we've talked about doing that someday. Why not now?"

I suppose there have been a few times in my life when someone's suggestion instantly resonated with me, but none—absolutely none—struck me as that one did. I didn't leap out of my chair—but almost. I looked around the table at that moment and responded emphatically, "Yes! That's exactly what we should do!"

Those words planted the seed of what was to become a small church planting movement, producing five more churches (as of this writing, with a sixth right around the corner), hundreds and hundreds of souls added to the kingdom of God, and nearly three thousand more people added to the fold. All that as a result of my wanting something bigger, . . . and (thank God) not getting my own way. Whether selling the church or selling something to the church, if the Lord is not in the pitch, it's a strikeout every time.

How good is God despite our mess-ups? Even in our blunders; our screwups; and yes, our sins, He never ceases to be at work, governing all situations in the direction of glorifying Himself. Job, at the point of wondering whether God had perhaps checked out of his life, made a profound observation:

> Behold, I go forward, but he is not there,
> and backward, but I do not perceive him;
> on the left hand *when he is working*, I do not behold him;
> he turns to the right hand, but I do not see him.
> But he knows the way that I take;
> when he has tried me, I shall come out as gold
> (Job 23:8–10, emphasis mine).

Did you catch that? Even when Job could not see God at work, he did not deny Him. Even when we don't see God, He is still *working*.

Within an hour of my spiritual epiphany, believing that God was leading us to plant a church, I called Dave Heisterkamp, the former Pastor of Administration at Saylorville Church. I had been his pastor and mentor, and when he came on staff we had become close friends.

Since his seminary days, Dave had dreamed of planting a church. When he came on staff, I asked him to stay at Saylorville for three to five years, and then we would consider church planting. He gave me a year and a half. Chomping at the bit to lead a church in his own right, and with Saylorville not even close to considering church planting, he left to pastor a small but established church about a hundred miles away.

By the time of my gymnasium disappointment and subsequent vision to plant a church, Dave had been pastoring for three years in the other church. While experiencing great success in applying his evangelistic abilities, he was also experiencing strong opposition from old-school traditionalists. What's more, he had just shared with his wife that they needed to pray about a possible change, because "something needs to give."

In my call to Dave I wasted no words: "How would you like to come back and plant a church with us?" I asked. He told me that he and his wife had been praying and shared that he immediately sensed this to be God's answer. As we hung up the phone that afternoon, we both knew God was up to something way bigger *and better* than a gymnasium. Truthfully, my dream had been too small!

A few years earlier, Ross, a friend of mine, had challenged me to think big—bigger than the way I was currently thinking, anyway. Ross told a crazy story of something that had happened to him, powerfully illustrating the point of dreaming too small. A solid baseball player, he had made the varsity team at Iowa State University. His first start would be against Oklahoma in Norman. He was beyond excited, and the night before the game he had a dream so real that he told his roommate about it before the game. He described in detail how he got a hit his first time up to the plate. He smacked the ball down the right-field line, rounded first base, and ended up with a stand-up double. As dreams go, this one had seemed incredibly real.

Imagine Ross's excitement when the game began and the actual moment of his first at-bat arrived. He stepped up and hit the ball—you've got it—straight down the right-field line. He roared past first base and made it to second for a stand-up double—exactly as he had dreamed! But his "dream come true" moment was quickly dashed when, arriving safely at second base, he looked up to see all his coaches and teammates yelling and stomping and waving at him. Everyone, that is, except his roommate, who knew exactly why he had stopped at second base. *He* was sitting in the dugout, legs crossed and smiling. As it turned out, Ross told me later, he could have easily made third base for a triple without even sliding. Why hadn't he gone on to third base? Because his dream had taken him only to second.

> MY DREAM HAD BEEN TO BUILD A GYMNASIUM. GOD'S DREAM WAS TO START A MOVEMENT.

My dream had been to build a gymnasium. God's dream was to start a movement. I wanted a bigger church. God wanted a bigger gospel impact. I wanted a place to play. God wanted His church to grow by starting other churches. My bigger was not better. It wasn't nearly big enough.

CULTIVATING HUMILITY

How big are *your* dreams? Is your bigger really *better*? To put it more plainly, do your passions really please the Lord? Stop selling the church and pitching your programs! If you take the time to study the Bible and learn what a New Testament church should be like, you will be refreshed and encouraged. The church that honors Christ will not need to be sold; rather, it will sell itself.

I'm not a car guy, but as the dad of ten kids I've learned a few things about buying and selling used cars. When it comes time to part company with most used cars, you have to *sell* them. You must highlight certain aspects of the car that might attract someone, while hoping they will overlook its drawbacks.

But there are used cars that are so attractive they almost sell themselves.

For instance, I recently owned a used vehicle I needed to sell. The car looked nice and ran well, but its nonfunctional parts and salvage title discouraged a number of people from purchasing it. Eventually it sold, but not before I had dropped the price and crossed my fingers (*I mean prayed!* about it).

At the same time, I have a friend with an amazing ability to build cars from scratch. He literally, from the frame up, builds classic cars with parts from the early seventies. He even restores and repaints every nut and bolt! His vehicles are not only hot items for classic car buyers but all turn out stunningly beautiful. With almost no effort on his part, buyers line up to bid on them.

Some things just sell themselves.

A Christ-honoring church should be like that—it should sell itself. Acts 2:41—6:7 lays out the essentials of a church, beautiful from the frame up.

The Christ-honoring church:

1. Regularly sees people come to Jesus. (2:47)
2. Regularly sees people identifying with Jesus in baptism. (2:41)
3. Regularly worships around the Word of God, the ordinances of God, and the people of God. (2:42, 46)
4. Generally conveys a spirit of awe from seeing miraculously changed lives. (2:43)
5. Regularly seeks to meet the needs of one another. (2:44-45)
6. Is known for its joy, generosity, and praise to God. (2:46-47)

7. Makes clear that the glory of changed lives belongs to Jesus. (3:12–16)

8. Knows that its power comes through the filling of the Holy Spirit, fasting, and prayer. (4:1–31; see also 13:2–3)

9. Practices church discipline with unrepentant sinners. (5:1–11; see also Matthew 18:15–17)

10. Raises up godly leaders from within the church. (6:1–7)

If your church doesn't do the things mentioned above, you might want to reconsider why you are there. It might be that the members *believe* those things but don't act upon them. If that's the case, then the church needs to be rebuilt—right down to the nuts and bolts being removed, restored, and repainted. There is another word for that. It's called *revival*, and there are many churches that desperately need to be revived. A friend who leads a large mission agency recently told me, "Pat, I've been in hundreds of churches that, on paper, believe exactly what you and I believe but don't preach the gospel on any given Sunday." Sadly, these are the churches that often sell lesser aspects of their ministries to get folks to buy in to their products. Their efforts might result in a bigger church, but they will never be a better church. Not one that honors Christ.

Don't sell the church. If yours is honoring God, you won't have to.

SCRIPTURES FOR MEDITATION

Isaiah 30:1; 31:1; Habakkuk 1:5; Acts 2:41–47; Ephesians 5:10; 1 Timothy (the whole book, but see particularly 1 Timothy 3:15)

CHAPTER 7

PULPIT SINS

"Why would anybody ever name their kid Jacob?"

Yes, I said that *from the pulpit*: "Why would anybody ever name their kid Jacob?" Looking back, my natural inclination is to give the statement context so that it doesn't sound quite as bad. But, even in its rightful context, I shouldn't have said it. Besides, I didn't just make the statement—*I yelled it.* More to come on this later in the chapter . . .

The average sermon delivered at my church is approximately 5,250 plus words long and takes about 35 minutes to preach. The same sermon is preached three times every Sunday morning, and I preach around 45 Sundays a year, so that comes to about 708,750 words annually. That also means that, in twenty years of my preaching at the same church, our folks have heard approximately 14,175,000 words proceed from my lips. That's a lot of words, and a lot of opportunities for mistakes; faux pas; and, yes, . . . *sins.* By sins, I mean things that are either unwise, wrong, or hurtful. To my shame, I have been guilty of all of the above.

During a Christmas series in my earlier years at Saylorville Church, I made another unwise statement. I was preaching on the first chapter of Luke, where the angel Gabriel appeared to the priest Zechariah in the temple. As you might recall, Zechariah and his wife, Elizabeth, were childless at the time, and Zechariah had been praying for a child, despite the fact he and his wife were getting older and Elizabeth was beyond the flower of her youth. As a priest, Zechariah's turn had come to offer incense, which, providentially, symbolized the prayers of His people going up to God. Suddenly, God's number one angel, Gabriel, appeared before Zechariah! He announced that Zechariah and Elizabeth would have a son who would become the very forerunner of the Christ. Amazing!

However, rather than lifting his voice in thanks and praise, Zechariah then asked if Gabriel might condescend to give him a sign! Try to imagine the moment. An angel of God—and not just any angel—appears before Zechariah. He reveals to him that his prayers have been both heard and answered. Then Zechariah has the audacity to ask for a sign—with the *sign* standing right in front of him! Here's how Luke records Gabriel's reply:

> "I am Gabriel! I stand in the presence of God. And I was sent to speak to you and to bring you this good news. And behold, you will be silent and unable to speak until the day that these things take place, because you did not believe my words, which will be fulfilled in their time" (Luke 1:19–20).

Now try to imagine my attempt to capture the reaction of Gabriel, who was clearly ticked. To grab the attention of my audience, I blurted a provocative line that had come to mind during my sermon preparation. I had known immediately that the statement would be edgy, but at the time I thought I needed to be edgy to drive home Gabriel's passionate reaction to Zechariah's unbelief. Hence, I inserted the line right into my notes: "Are you *freakin'* kidding me?! I am Gabriel." Some of you reading this may be thinking, *What's the big deal? People use that word all the time.* But in those days that word was *not* used all the time; that's what made it so edgy during the first few years of this millennium. I'd had a few human filters around me during my sermon preparation, and I could have bounced that line off them before saying it in public, but I didn't. And I did have one friend who had actually cautioned me against saying it.

Regrettably, I ignored him.

But there was Someone else I ignored, which made it even worse. As I wrote the line into my notes, I sensed the Holy Spirit warning me against going through with it. I really did. I wrestled back and forth, wondering if that hesitation was from God or just my being too "chicken" to use the word. We are warned by God in 1 Thessalonians 5:19 not to "quench the Spirit," meaning "Don't ignore His promptings."

Sadly, that's exactly what I did.

The mistake I made that day did more than embarrass me; it humiliated me. The statement offended several of our people who immediately recognized it as a kind of "replacement swear word," utterly inappropriate in the moment. Hence, a sermon intended to challenge God's people toward obedience and holiness was hijacked by a line several could not get off their minds.

That week the Holy Spirit, gracious as He is, did not give up on me. He troubled my spirit over what I had said. No one had directly challenged my statement. I received no emails or phone calls or personal visits. But the staff—much smaller then—did have a field day with it. Whenever a statement was made that someone else strongly disagreed with, the line was jokingly repeated. Our technology manager even recorded the remark, along with a few other embarrassing public comments I'd made in those early years. (He later went on to create a ringtone of my faux pas!) Though this was humorous, and not meant to hurt, my conscience was deeply troubled before God.

I later wrote an email to the church family asking their forgiveness for my having said what I did. I wish I could tell you I never again made another public blunder like this. That, unfortunately, would not be true. There would be more pulpit sins to come, and with each blunder more lessons to learn and retractions to make.

PUBLIC SINS REQUIRE PUBLIC CONFESSION

One Sunday night at Saylorville during the teaching time with around three hundred adults in the room, I impressed upon our people the necessity of daily Bible reading and all the spiritual benefits that come from it. At the end I asked the congregation for a show of hands as to who would commit to reading their Bibles before leaving their homes each day. As expected, many hands went up. As I looked around I saw, just off to the left side and sitting in the front, an old friend and longtime member of the church. As our eyes met, I noticed that he was not one who raised his hand. Instinctively (that might have been the problem), I spoke directly to him: "Bob! Why aren't you raising your hand? Of all people here, you know the importance of daily Bible reading." I was half joking with him, but only *half*. Bob caught the serious side of my open comment, but he neither smiled in agreement nor raised his hand. This was not going over well. I'd gone from teaching publicly to picking out one individual and having an off-the-cuff dialogue with him—but he wasn't dialoguing! The awkwardness could be felt throughout the room. I sheepishly smiled and finished up my final thoughts before closing the service.

The next day I called Bob. I acknowledged the foolishness of my calling him out and assuming he would play along. I then asked his forgiveness. Bob, exceedingly gracious, forgave me. He also explained why he didn't raise his hand. He reminded me that a promise to God is a sacred thing (Ecclesiastes 5:4–5) and that, while he desired to read his Bible every day, he simply wasn't ready to publicly say so. I acknowledged his humble words and assured him that I would clear this up by confessing my wrong the very next Sunday. Bob didn't think this necessary, but I knew it was.

The next Sunday night I openly asked Bob, sitting in the same spot as the week before, for his forgiveness for my foolish assumption and for pressing him as I had done. He kindly nodded, mouthing the words, "I do forgive you." Suddenly the awkward atmosphere, so thick the week before, became free—even joyful.

The silver lining to my blunder occurred about two months later. The leadership interviewed a couple for church membership. They had recently moved to our area and had visited several Bible-believing churches. They liked our church but liked another one as well. We asked them what had helped them come to a final decision, and they went on to tell us that they were in attendance the night I asked Bob to forgive me publicly. "We've been worshiping in good churches for many years but have never witnessed a pastor publicly asking for forgiveness from anyone. We knew that night that this was the church for us."

Cool.

However, none of my other pulpit sins can rival the one that shocked our entire church. I still shudder to think I ever made such a statement, unintentionally hurting folks I truly love.

Here's what happened: I was preaching in the book of Genesis, sharing the story of Jacob and Esau, the fraternal twin sons of Isaac and Rebekah. In those days, parents often named their children in accordance with the circumstances surrounding the nation; times; personal plights; or, in as the cases of Jacob and Esau, their actual births. Genesis 25 records their fascinating story. Esau, who came out first, was full of hair; hence, his parents named him Esau, meaning "hairy."

On the other hand, the circumstances of Jacob's birth were quite unusual. We are told in Scripture that he and his twin, Esau, had struggled together in the womb. In fact, when it came time for the twins to be born, "Esau came out first, with his brother holding on to his heel, as if to say, "Get back in here! I'm not done with you!" Isaac named his second-born Jacob, meaning "heal-grabber." The meaning conveys the idea of one who sneaks up from behind and trips up another, like the schoolyard trick a bully might play on another boy.

Later, the name Jacob became synonymous with "deceiver." Jacob spent most of his life living up (or, better said, living *down*) to his name as a conniving trickster. Years later, when Jacob wrestled with God, the Lord made Jacob come to terms with his own folly and confess his dishonest life. Only after this admission did God change his name to Israel, meaning "God contends." No longer would Jacob fight by his own wits and deception. He would come to the God Who fights his battles.

As I zeroed in on the meaning of Jacob's name and how he lived in accordance with it, I raised the tenor of my voice and then asked incredulously, "Why would anybody ever name their kid Jacob?!" I must have sounded mad (as in insane) at that moment. We had at least four or five Jacobs in our church. What was I thinking? That's just it—I wasn't.

When I came to my senses over the next day or two, I made a few personal calls. I even wrote a letter to the church family, expressing my sorrow and repentance for such an insensitive and hurtful remark. I also made a call to a couple I had personally evangelized a few years earlier. They were particularly hurt, and rightly so. Thankfully, I found them, as well as the rest of God's people, incredibly forgiving.

ILLUSTRATIONS

Pulpit and other public sins can even occur in the form of a well-intended illustration gone awry. One illustration I gave early in my preaching experience crossed the line of what is appropriate and is my earliest personal recollection of verbal buffoonery. Believe me, it was a doozy.

During a message I preached on evangelism in 1989, I tried to illustrate the importance of getting on the level of the person you hope to reach for Christ, as Paul instructed us in 1 Corinthians 9. For impact and integrity, I regularly incorporate recent experiences in my sermons. To this day, our congregation regularly hears me say "Just the other day" before sharing an illustration. Current experiences illustrating biblical truth tell God's people the speaker is staying current with God and men. I also stress this truth to younger pastors I mentor. But just because the story is a current one doesn't make it the appropriate one. Unfortunately, the recent experience I shared that day would become famous or, more accurately, infamous. Disastrous best describes this illustration.

Our newborn son had just been circumcised. (I know. Flashing red lights should have been going off in my head, as they are in yours right now.) As I contemplated how to best illustrate the need for relating to people when sharing Jesus with them, I remembered our boy's checkup earlier that week. I told the church how our doctor, after thoroughly examining our little guy, looked up at me and, rather than using scientific, medical terminology to describe what he saw, simply stated, "Well, his pee-pee looks good!"

Hilarious, right?

Wrong.

I hoped for laughter but heard only silence in that little country church. Dead silence. I did *see* a few things. Faces. Stunned faces, as in "I can't believe you just said that!" The only thing worse than the illustration itself was the fact that I had 15 minutes left to preach. I would have been better off shutting it down then and there. Believe me when I reflect that few things are more painful for a preacher than preaching while actively thinking of a major faux pas made earlier in the message. The rest of the sermon circled the drain, then drew to a close.

IF YOU'RE QUESTIONING WHETHER SOMETHING IS APPROPRIATE TO SAY, IT PROBABLY ISN'T.

My failed public words have two things in common: (1) I ignored the Holy Spirit's warning, and (2) I failed to hear godly human filters who may have prevented me from sharing the ill-advised illustration. One has to be willing to submit to these filters. This truism is worth following: If you're questioning whether something is appropriate to say, it probably isn't.

EMBELLISHMENTS

This next story illustrates the importance of *accuracy*. I actually came out looking okay on this one, . . . but just barely. Rabih Alameddine, a Lebanese American painter and writer, said, "Show me a storyteller who doesn't embellish, and I'll show you a bad one." An intriguing line, . . . bearing in mind that there can be a very fine one between embellishment and lying. An accusation of both came nearly fifty years after the incident I had shared one Easter Sunday. What's more, the accusation related to a story I have been telling for over thirty years, a story that would come back to haunt me. And it all began on the football field in the sixth grade.

Sixth grade—does anybody remember sixth grade? I don't remember much. I do remember winning my first city wrestling championship at—wait for it—75 pounds. I actually went on to capture the 82-pound and 92-pound championships to finish out my middle-school days. Those were great memories. Wrestling became my sport of choice throughout my high-school years, and I even qualified for the Iowa State High School Wrestling Tournament my senior year.

Football, however, was always my first love, though I never excelled in the sport. In my day, playing with helmets and pads didn't start until sixth grade.

The year was 1970. At 75 pounds, I wore a helmet that was too big for my head and pads and pants two sizes too big. I was blissfully ignorant of those details because football had begun, and I couldn't have been more excited.

I desperately wanted to be a quarterback. I ended up as a halfback and joined a group of five or six other would-be halfbacks. One day our coach set up a real helmet-and-pad-smacking tackling drill. We halfbacks lined up, one behind the other, and to our left, at a ninety-degree angle, stood the tacklers. The objective? To outrun the tacklers and get to the standing dummy as they came at us from the side.

These drills never went well for the runners, especially if their fate was to meet up with Pat Dunlay. Pat, who gave me permission to share this story, was not only two years older than me but one of the meanest guys in school. As I mentally numbered off us runners and those tacklers, I suddenly realized I was going to face him! I literally began to tremble. Then, in no more than the few seconds it took to consider how I might survive the upcoming collision, I felt a tap on my shoulder pad. It was the guy behind me —believe it or not, he was even smaller than me. As though oblivious to the guy he'd be attempting to outrun, he offered, "I can go ahead of you." I couldn't believe it. It was as though the football gods were suddenly smiling down upon me. Covering up my obvious delight, I responding with something profound like "Okay."

The moments that followed were traumatic. We all heard the *crack*. The scream. The commotion. Clear, distinct lines of stunned halfbacks and tacklers suddenly circled around my friend as he lay on the ground, writhing in pain from a terribly broken shoulder. Everyone was shocked, but none more than me.

Our coach, a loud, tough disciplinarian, suddenly turned nurse. He took a knee near the boy and quickly discerned the seriousness of the situation. When he realized the rest of us were just standing there, mouths open in horror and staring at the victim, he snapped, "Laps! All of you! Start running laps!"

More than willing, we ran. Since we all knew the normal pattern of running the school field, we took off around the oval. Why mention that? Because the normal oval pattern took us right past the location where the accident had occurred. One lap, two, three, then four. And every time we ran by the scene, I saw my friend on the ground in excruciating pain. Each time we crossed his path, I thought, *That should have been me. He took my place.*

This illustration about that long-ago day at football practice is one of the first I ever shared from the pulpit in the little country church I pastored. As our congregation observed the Lord's Table, I told this story, making the analogy to the story of Jesus and what He did for us. Just as I had thought every time I ran past my hurting friend, *He took my place,* so every time we come to the Lord's Table we must remember, *Jesus took our place—on the cross.* While we deserved to pay for our own sins, God "laid on him the iniquity of us all" (Isaiah 53:6). As my friend suffered in my place, so Jesus died in our place (1 Peter 3:18). His pain became our gain. His suffering opened the way for our salvation. This illustration has deeply impacted God's people over the years.

In case you were wondering, my friend eventually recovered from his injuries, but his football days were over. His wrestling days, however, were still to come. Like me, he wrestled, and, also like me, he was a good wrestler. Unlike me, he became an outstanding wrestler. He would go on to accomplish more than I ever did on the mat. However, some five or six years later he had to default a big match due to reinjuring his shoulder. He didn't hurt it on the same level as in the original accident, but the reinjury was clearly the result of what had happened years earlier in the sixth grade. I felt as though I had done that to him all over again.

So, what does this story have to do with *accuracy* in telling our stories? Fast forward 48 years. While I was preaching an Easter series, an opportunity presented itself for me to share the story again. My old friend whose shoulder had been injured at practice many years earlier had moved to my town. I decided to reach out to him through private social media. A few years earlier I had comforted him when a member of his family had died, so we had at least made some connection after so many years. I now invited him to visit our church to hear me tell a story from our youth that included him. That made him curious, and he said he would come to hear me preach. I couldn't have been more excited. I hoped to take him out for lunch or coffee afterward. As it turned out, he never showed up. Though disappointed, I didn't show it. I communicated with him a day or two later in an effort to keep the invite open. A week went by. Then two. Still no response.

Finally, three weeks later, he responded.

Imagine my shock when I read, "I listened to your sermon, and I think you owe your congregation an apology for lying to them."

I couldn't believe it. Was he joking? The next line told me he wasn't.

"I never tapped you on the shoulder to go ahead of you. You *pushed* me ahead of you."

I sat back, absolutely flabbergasted! But he wasn't finished. "And that tackler wasn't the meanest guy in town. He was a super nice guy—not mean at all. It bothers me that you lied in God's house. Lying to *embellish* your story is wrong. NO! I won't be attending your services."

In that moment, I'd like to say that you could have knocked me over with a feather, but that would be an embellishment. Stunned, I wondered, *Could I have gotten the story so wrong?*

I mean, I get it. Forty-eight years is a long time, and if you tell a story the same way for thirty years, right or wrong, that version *becomes* your reality. I shared the story the way it had *come down,* whether or not that was the way it had *gone down.* In any case, my friend was not only upset, he was clearly bitter against me—nearly fifty years after the fact.

As it turns out, corroboration can be a wonderful thing. And, believe it or not, I received confirmation of my story even after five decades. My very best friend and fellow sixth grader was a kid named Dennis Dunlay. He became my best man in my first marriage. To this very day, we talk and usually make time to get together with our wives every year for old times' sake. And if you're wondering if his last name sounds familiar, it should. The "mean guy" who broke my other friend's shoulder was Dennis's brother! As it turned out, Dennis was not only at the scene of the supposed crime that day as a witness, but the memory of it was so traumatic and vivid that not even he forgot any of the details. I asked Dennis after receiving the bitter response from our friend whether it were possible I had indeed gotten it all wrong. Dennis corroborated my story, even agreeing that his brother had been mean in those days (though he is a nice guy today). Most importantly, he remembered our friend volunteering to take my place. I mean, what are the odds of all that?

Now what should I do? I had told a story publicly but was later utterly rebuked by someone in the story for having told a lie to God's people. Then I was vindicated by my friend who had witnessed the whole thing.

Before I tell you what I did, let me hit the pause button. In this case, there were two "buttons" my injured friend pushed in his response to me; both gave me pause before I could think about defending myself. I had been accused of two sins: *lying* and *embellishing.* I know what you're thinking: *Aren't they the same thing?* On one level, yes. Lying is lying. To lie is to deliberately state an untruth, whereas embellishing is more distorting the truth. When you think about it, both are wrong. Embellishing, especially for preachers, can sometimes fall into the category of hyperbole (exaggeration), which is an acceptable form of communication. However, this can be a fine line to walk.

My offended friend and I briefly communicated back and forth, but it didn't seem to help. I appealed to him based on my invitation. Why would I even have thought to invite him if I had been planning to lie and distort the truth about something so traumatic in his life? Why would I have planned to lie or embellish the story with him sitting in attendance at the church I pastor? That made no sense, but I realized it was probably a good thing he hadn't come. He might've called me out as a liar in front of the whole church. A certain segment of the church might have enjoyed that—not because they would have believed him but just to have witnessed their pastor's response!

I finally conceded to my friend that, regardless of who remembered correctly, I had been wrong at the time of the incident. Push or no push way back there in the sixth grade, I had known whom my friend would be facing. Willing or unwilling, he had still taken my place and paid a very heavy price.

CULTIVATING HUMILITY

If your area of service in the church involves pastoring, counseling, or teaching (adults, youth, or children), you're telling stories. If your line of work outside the church is in management, human resources, social work, marketing, business, or finance, you're also telling stories. If you're a parent, you're definitely telling stories. Regardless of your life's calling, you need to be able to tell a story well. Whether or not you speak from an actual platform, most of us have a figurative platform from which we speak. Let's strive to avoid *public sins*—since telling a story also requires truthfulness. Some considerations to keep in mind:

> MOST PUBLIC SINS START IN OUR HEART. THE GOOD NEWS IS THAT WE HAVE AN ADVOCATE DWELLING WITHIN TO HELP US.

1. Aim toward accuracy.

   Pastors are storytellers. Few of us are exempt from embellishing our stories, myself included. The day my friend accused me of embellishing his story caused me to think twice from then on about the accuracy of stories I tell, as well as about the people who might be impacted by them.

2. Expect to be misunderstood.

   Even when you're humble, you will be misunderstood. Our fallen world will not always respond kindly to the stories we tell. Accept this as fact and move on.

3. Get permission when naming names.

   It is wise whenever possible to seek permission to use another person's name when you tell a story involving them. Otherwise, simply don't use their name or choose a pseudonym in the place of their name.

4. Be humble when you mess up.

   If you're a public speaker, you're bound to make public mistakes. When your mistake—your pulpit or public sin—comes to light, own it. Don't make the situation worse by making excuses. If you do, the matter might pass, but the memory of your unwillingness to face your blunder will not be forgotten.

5. Listen to the Holy Spirit in the process.

    Most public sins start in our heart. The good news is that we have an Advocate dwelling within to help us. Do not ignore the Holy Spirit, either when He urges you to say something or when He urges you *not* to say something. "Do not quench the Spirit" (1 Thessalonians 5:19).

6. Seek forgiveness from those you've offended.

    Remember that, when you blow it publicly, God's people tend to be incredibly forgiving. Why? Because they themselves have been forgiven. What's more, as God loves humility, so do His people—generally, that is. Believe it or not, when you openly confess your public sins, your esteem from God's people will not go down, but up.

SCRIPTURES FOR MEDITATION

Proverbs 28:13; Matthew 6:14–15; Ephesians 4:30; James 3:1; 1 Peter 5:6-7; 1 John 1:9–10

CHAPTER 8

HOW TO SEE IN THE DARK

"He uncovers the deeps out of darkness
and brings deep darkness to light."
JOB 12:22

Some things are seen only in the dark. Some of the things we need to retract, remove, and repent of are revealed to us only when we are in a dark place. For me, that dark place was the day my wife died.

Nina was the light of my life. We met in chemistry class during my junior year in high school, but the *chemistry* wasn't working—at least not for her. I was smitten from the start, but our first date didn't come until the next summer on my seventeenth birthday. Funny, the only part of the date I remember was the end of it. Nina literally had the door of my red 1968 Volkswagen Beetle open before it came to a complete stop in her parents' driveway! Later she explained, "You had a *reputation* with the girls."

True.

Somehow, God, with His sovereign plan in mind, finally brought us together. We married three years later, and a year and a half after that we started a family. Three years into our marriage we became Christians. The Lord worked first on my heart before transforming Nina's. She later testified to having been frightened by the changes in me as, one after another, I brought home gospel books, booklets, or tracts for reading. As for the Bible, we didn't even own one. I borrowed a Bible from my mother-in-law, who, at the time, found my interest a positive thing. And Nina? She was counting the cost of what her husband's newfound spiritual interest might bring to the already struggling marriage. She figured she would ride this thing out to see whether any good might come from it.

> SOME THINGS ARE SEEN ONLY IN THE DARK. SOME OF THE THINGS WE NEED TO RETRACT, REMOVE, AND REPENT OF ARE REVEALED TO US ONLY WHEN WE ARE IN A DARK PLACE.

On September 6, 1982, at 12:30 a.m, the *good* came. I was converted to Christ. After nearly two years of my hearing the gospel, reading gospel materials, and weighing the input I had taken in, God humbled my heart. I repented of my sins and received Jesus as my Savior. With my heart and destiny changed, I found peace, but our home became a spiritual war zone. My salvation literally struck fear in Nina's heart. She wondered, *What's happened to my husband?*

Two weeks after my conversion, my brother Mike, who had led me to Christ, invited us to travel three hours by car to visit the church he was leading. As the pastor, he hoped to introduce us to his church, particularly the folks who had been praying for us. I hoped and prayed that Nina would respond to the loving witness of my brother and his wife, but that almost didn't happen. Just one day before our trip, Nina spoke up and voiced aloud what she had been thinking: "I never said I was going. You can go if you want. Not me." I felt hurt and upset; the scene wasn't pretty. I called my brother to tell him that Nina now refused to go. As it turned out, he and his wife were having a Bible study at that very moment.

Their study suddenly became a prayer meeting, and God listened in! Before long Nina's heart began to soften. She agreed to make the trip, but the battle for her soul was on. As Jesus once said, "No one can come to me unless the Father who sent me draws him" (John 6:44). God was indeed drawing Nina, but her lost soul resisted Him until she could do so no longer. Her war with God ceased that Sunday evening as she listened to my brother preach the gospel in his church. Mike preached from 1 Thessalonians 4. He affirmed everything I had come to believe two weeks earlier and had shared with Nina, who sat quietly in the pew, taking it all in. I had no idea how the message was impacting her, but it wasn't long before I found out.

That night, during our long drive home, we sat quietly, thinking over the events and the message of the day. The next morning Nina approached me with tears in her eyes. She told me that during the trip home she had spoken with Jesus, confessed her sin, and placed her faith in Him. What joy that brought to our lives and marriage! Now, truly one spiritually, we could go forward as one. For us, that was *fast*-forward!

Among a thousand experiences in the next 13 years, God blessed us with six more children, a Bible college degree, and the call to Holmes Baptist Church in northcentral Iowa. As we started our ninth year, the church enjoyed an amazing time of

> GOD LOVES TO TEST OUR FAITH. IF THE RESULTS OF THE TEST DO NOT HAVE A WOW! ATTACHED TO THEM, THEN IT'S NOT MUCH OF A TEST.

growth with an extraordinary capital campaign, raising, without borrowing, monies equaling three times what had been the church's annual income. I led the church to trust God to bring the monies in, and, through what seemed like miraculous circumstances, He provided it all. The incredible test of our church's faith resulted in great joy and praise to God. Even the community outside our church was marveling over what God was doing. I wrote in my journal during that time, "God loves to test our faith. If the results of the test do not have a *Wow!* attached to them, then it's not much of a test."

Unbeknownst to me, on the wings of passing this great test, God began preparing me for the greatest test of my life. This test revealed weaknesses in my walk I had never before realized.

MY MIDNIGHT

As I think about Nina, I'm reminded of a time we heard Elisabeth Elliot speak at a conference. Her standup microphone kept swinging away from her, and she kept pulling it back, to the annoyance of the audience, myself included. Her husband, Lars, suddenly walked down the aisle, took hold of the mic, and started fixing the problem. Meanwhile, he asked Elisabeth, as she waited for him to get the mic fixed, to tell the audience about her second husband. "Nobody ever hears about him," he said. We all roared with laughter. Elisabeth, as though on cue, spoke affectionately about Addison Leach, the second husband "nobody ever heard about." We loved it, never thinking the story would ever relate to our lives.

What can I say about Nina, my first wife, my lover, my best friend, my source of strength, and the period at the end of each day? Not an extraordinary person by the world's standards, she was quiet, attractive, always pleasant, patient, godly, and theologically as steady as a rock. That's how she presented herself. As a mother of seven children, ages fourteen down to one, the baby just weaned, she stayed incredibly busy. She homeschooled the four older children while keeping our home clean, orderly, and happy. When the burden of all these accountabilities started to weigh on her in early 1995, Psalm 61:2 lifted her up: "When my heart is faint, lead me to the rock that is higher than I." I can still picture her standing up during a testimony time at an evening service to share how the Lord used that Scripture to comfort her. I remember because she rarely put herself forward like that.

The summer of '95 was one of the hottest in years. In July, I took my 14-year-old with me on a high school canoe trip in Minnesota where I spoke to teenagers along the banks of the Crow Wing River. Nina stayed home with our other six children. In fact, she even took in a couple of other kids from our church family who needed a babysitter.

That was Nina.

We returned from our youth trip on Friday, and I had never seen Nina so glad to have me back home. Nina did not fret, nor was she a woman given to worry, but I still remember how my leaving this time had actually brought her to tears. Her fears, she said, were not for herself but for me. She expressed an almost unbearable fear of losing me, but she didn't ask me to stay home. Instead, she insisted she was "just being silly" and encouraged us to go. Still, when I returned home safely, she was absolutely thrilled and relieved.

The following evening, I received a phone call from a woman whose grandfather was in the hospital with a serious heart condition. She asked me to pray for him and his recovery. Of course, I said I would, but I also reminded her that she had a responsibility to share Jesus with her grandfather and urged her to do so. I still remember quoting Proverbs 27:1 to her, a passage that warns, "Do not boast about tomorrow, for you do not know what a day may bring," reminding her of the sobering fact that her grandfather might not have a tomorrow. I had no clue that those very truthful words, communicated to her in what may have been a less than compassionate way, would in only a few hours come to rest upon me.

One of the retractions the Lord produced in me that night and in the following days was to quit glibly sharing inexperienced truth with those who hurt. I didn't *think* I had done that, but, as I look back, I have to acknowledge that my counsel sometimes, though truthful, lacked the compassion appropriate for the given moment. Every pastor must teach, preach, and minister to those who suffer in ways he has not, and we must in those times proceed gently, humbly, and yet truthfully with those in the depths of a trial. Experience or no experience, we must be truth-tellers. But if we have not lived what those individuals are experiencing, we must also humbly acknowledge that lack of experience to the sufferer.

That acknowledgment helps them swallow the pills they are about to take.

The rest of the evening continued as usual in our home. We ate as a family, played, then had a devotional time from the children's devotional *Keys for Kids*. As God would have it, the devotion that very day included a nature story about the Jack Pine tree. The seeds from a Jack Pine do not release unless exposed to great heat, such as a forest fire. Then, once released, they reseed the burned-out ground. The "key" from the devotional was that we *grow in trials*. The lesson that evening foreshadowed one the children and I would learn over time.

After Nina and I prayed with our children, we kissed each one, told them we loved them, and sent them to bed. The very last words our children heard from their mother were that she loved them.

With the kids asleep, we sat on the couch experiencing a sweet, loving, and even romantic time together. After a kiss, I remember Nina's final words to me: "I missed you so much."

Suddenly, and completely out of the blue, she gasped and slumped into my arms. Though momentarily shocked, I knew immediately that something was wrong—terribly wrong. Nina was unresponsive; looking back, I am one-hundred percent certain she was gone from that instant.

The next few minutes became hours filled with shock, horror, and instinctive reactions: Calling 911. Calling our sweet neighbor, a nurse, who came right away. The ambulance. The trip to the hospital. The doctor who had delivered five of our children, in tears, pronouncing Nina's death. Embraces from many at the small community hospital where we had doctored for nearly a decade. Then the heartbreaking quiet, the numbness, and the trip back home in the backseat of a friend's car—alone.

I had been widowed for just a few hours, and I remember, for the first time, feeling lonely.

Then there were our children—asleep through it all, unaware of what had just happened. The time was about 3:00 a.m, but my personal midnight had just begun. I hadn't even cried yet, though I had cried out to God to bring Nina back; He had answered *No*.

The uncontrollable crying came soon enough. The most difficult task of my life lay ahead: telling our children. The knowledge of their mother's death would be just too deep for our younger ones to comprehend. I remember one of them looking around, confused, before going back to playing with some toy. But news of their mommy's death devastated our older two.

Our oldest, Sarah, at 14, was beyond her years in maturity—her mother had trained her well. The two of them had done everything together, with Sarah apprenticing at Nina's side. I knew I had to start with her, and I knew I couldn't wait until morning. The time now was 3:30 a.m. I walked into her tiny bedroom at the top of the stairs. The space was meant to be a closet, but that mattered little to a 14-year-old who finally had her own room. I sat on the bed next to her. My heart was now heavy, so very heavy. Sound asleep, she looked at peace—so unprepared to hear and understand what had just happened. I sighed as never before, while stroking her long brown hair. "Sarah," I whispered quietly. "Sarah, you need to wake up, honey." She turned toward me on her side, eyes barely open and unsure of what was going on. The door to her room, partly open, allowed the light from the hallway to filter in, enough for us to see each other but not enough to startle her. The revelation itself would be startling enough. "Sarah, I have some very sad news to tell you."

Her eyes were opening, and her senses grew more alert.

"Sarah, I don't know how else to say this to you, honey. Your mommy just went to heaven." She suddenly sat up straight, her face in shock.

"What?!" I took her in my arms and, as best I could, explained what had just transpired.

Her sorrow was indescribable.

"Oh, Mommy! Oh, Mommy!" she repeated over and over, for how long I can't remember. I only recall holding her and weeping with her for a long time. To this day I weep every time I recall that heartrending moment—which I avoid doing any more often than I need to.

The reality is though, that I *do* need to.

The death of Nina produced a number of retractions in my life, and almost all of them had to do with my own lack of compassion.

There, I've said it.

I was not a very compassionate Christian, much less pastor. Don't misunderstand: I *thought* I was compassionate. If you had asked me before the day my wife died whether I was compassionate, I would have replied in the affirmative. I could easily have supplied a list of situations and circumstances in which I had demonstrated some semblance of compassion: multiple hospital calls and upholding those experiencing broken relationships, deaths of loved ones, and even births gone tragically wrong. In each case, I brought God's Word and its answers—His answers—to the moment. Without a doubt, the Lord used those moments to instill renewed hope into those who were hurting. I'm reminded that God, His Word, and His Spirit are more than enough to make up for failed empathy. They do not, however, provide a rationale for excusing a lack of real, visceral, heartfelt compassion.

SEEING IN THE DARK

The Lord did not waste any time humbling my less-than-compassionate heart. One week after Nina's death, He first used a preacher's gentle words to soften me. Then, days later, He used a note from the same little girl whose pathetic cry for her mommy still rang in my ears to demonstrate the power of real, heartfelt compassion. Sarah, still reeling from the sudden loss of her mom, turned away from her own sorrow to help me in mine. God used both that preacher and my daughter to help me to see in my darkness. And this all happened at camp.

Our attending a Christian family camp at that time may appear to have been strange. Why would a dad take his kids to a camp just a week after their mother's death? Our family had signed up to attend camp months earlier; this was to have been our family vacation that year. We were all excited about going, especially since I was not scheduled to speak during that week of camp. Normally, because of our lack of resources, we took advantage of summer speaking invitations I received from different camps, not only to minister but to give our kids a fun vacation. This was different. I had planned an undistracted week with Nina and the kids, apart from any speaking responsibilities.

Nina and I had saved enough money to secure the cheapest lodging in the camp—the Barn. Really, that's what they called it (apparently, at one time, it had actually been a barn.) All in all, it was *very* basic: one big room with lots of bunk beds—just right for a family of nine! We had been determined to make it work and had looked forward to our time at camp and all its fun activities. Then, just a week before our planned getaway, Nina left for heaven.

Honestly, with the blur of responsibilities surrounding Nina's death, I almost forgot about the anticipated vacation. When I did remember, I thought, *There's no way we're going to camp now.* Before I could cancel our reservation, however, the camp director called me, pleading with me to still come to camp with the kids. He offered to cover our cost, reasoning that camp would be a much-needed distraction for my hurting kids. His gracious offer instantly rang true, so I accepted. With heavy hearts, we were off to camp.

The guest speaker that week was an older pastor I had met once before during my college days. David Moore, the late pastor of Walnut Ridge Baptist Church in Waterloo, Iowa, was a man filled with the compassion of Christ. As soon as he heard the buzz that a young, suddenly widowed pastor was in attendance, he offered his sincere condolences. But God used the opening line of Pastor Moore's very first message to bring me to tears and show me the heart of Jesus. He looked across his audience and said, "Jesus anticipates the needs of His children."

With that statement, God opened every tear duct in my eyes. *Of course He does! My pain was no accident. It was anticipated!* How I loved that thought. Those words took me directly into the heart of our compassionate Savior by way of a compassionate preacher. Later I wondered, *Do I preach with such compassion?* The fact that I had to ask myself this painful question anticipated my answer.

A few nights later, after the kids had gone to sleep, I allowed myself another cry. Most nights were like this. I made every attempt to put on a show of strength for my brokenhearted kids throughout the day, but once they were asleep and I had some space, I let my tears flow. However, on this particular night at camp, I didn't have my usual space in which to cry. My kids were literally sleeping all around me. Even so, lying in my bed, wracked with loneliness and a dozen other emotions, I began to weep.

SO, HOW DID I LEARN TO BE COMPASSIONATE? BY BEING PUT INTO A DARK PLACE.

Unbeknownst to me, Sarah heard my weeping. The next morning I awoke to a note, written in the night by my 14-year-old daughter. In it she acknowledged having heard me cry and felt led to encourage me. She assured me that we would be okay. God would see us through this dark time. She ended with this verse from God's Word: "For it is you who light my lamp; the LORD my God lightens my darkness" (Psalm 18:28).

So, how did I learn to be compassionate? By being put into a dark place. For me, it took nothing less than the death of the love of my life. Yet there, in my own personal midnight, God, with compassionate words from a preacher and a daughter, began to shine His light into the dark crevices of my heart. Over time, as I brought God's promises and hope to those who were hurting, my own tears began to flow with and for those I was comforting.

And yes, I now thank God for the dark times in my life because there He gave me some of His greatest light.

CULTIVATING HUMILITY

As I wrote at the beginning of this chapter, some things are seen only in the dark. Are you in a dark place right now? It might be the very place in which the Lord wants to give you light. The truths God wants us to see in the dark are often our own character deficiencies. For me, the deficit was compassion. For you, it might be trusting in God or submitting to His ways in some area of your life. God might be using your dark place to reveal bad thinking or bad theology in your life (misinformation, like assuming that bad things happen only to bad people or some such foolishness). In any case, don't waste your darkness. God might be shedding some of His light on you.

God's Light in the Darkness

Here are just a few questions to ask yourself when you're in a dark place:

1. Have I actually done something to put myself here? Because we do reap what we sow (Galatians 6:7), each of us needs to give serious consideration to the possibility that we might be in a dark place based on our own doing. Confessing and forsaking a sin that put us there is no guarantee that we'll come out of the darkness anytime soon, but it will guarantee forgiveness and light within it.
2. What area of your character is God addressing in this dark place? As said, for me it was lack of compassion. What characteristics of Christ are you lacking? Is it possible God is using your dark place to help you see?
3. Who are the people God is using to shed light in your darkness? Have you thanked God for them? Have you thanked them?

SCRIPTURES FOR MEDITATION
Psalm 25; Daniel 2:22; John 8:12

CHAPTER 9

JOHN

Because your steadfast love is better than life,

my lips will praise you.

PSALM 63:3

first shared the verse above on July 23, 2011. That was the day
the wife of a young man from our church, a woman who had
battled cancer, finally succumbed to the disease. My hope for
him was that, even during his great sorrow, he might yet give
praise to God, whose lovingkindness was better than life itself.

This verse seemed to me to be a godly, loving, appropriate,
and pastoral reminder to give him at the time. My young friend,
now a widower with two little girls, embraced both the verse and
its meaning.

Not long thereafter, I would need to do the same.

As I wrote in the introduction, our two youngest boys
had become the bane of our existence during their high school
years, which happened to be at the same time as the sickness and
eventual death of the young wife and mother. Despite wonderful

things happening in ministry and church life, every day (and I do mean every day) I was struggling with regard to the lives, choices, actions, and very destinies of both Daniel and John. Through a series of circumstances, the Holy Spirit changed the heart of Daniel. This handsome high schooler had the looks and personality that caused the young ladies to swoon over him. That is, until one young lady he liked dumped him like a bad habit. He was devastated, and the result would be just what the Divine Doctor had ordered. Soon afterward, Daniel turned back to the Lord and has never looked back.

His brother John, however, remained resistant and determined to defy all authority—starting with me. The high school principal called regularly—by regularly, I mean three to five times a week. Added to that, John was also skipping out regularly from church by spending nights at his friends' homes on Saturdays. Conveniently, he would oversleep and not make it to church. Then, when he did come, he would usually fall asleep in the dimly lit back corner. I even pulled him from youth group because his influence was impacting other students in ways not conducive to their spirituality. One of his best friends' parents, although continuing to love and pray for him throughout all his rebellious years, realized that inviting him over would no longer be wise or healthy for their own children.

When he was little, John had been easy and compliant. He was so quiet he could go almost unnoticed around the house. Like most boys, he loved sports and loved to play. He also had lots of friends. Although his grades in school were never very good, he was not a problem child, . . . until, within just a short time, he became one. At first his quiet demeanor turned unresponsive, and he was increasingly darker. He started spending more time with questionable friends and less time with the ones who made better choices. We detected a growing anger inside him, but we were not sure how or when it would show up.

Then, when he was sixteen, it did.

One afternoon I looked outside to see a police squad car pull into our driveway. The officer came to our door and asked whether John was home. I remember my heart sinking in the moment. *What could John have done?* I thought. As it turned out, John was home, so we called for him. He came out of his room and met the officer, who kindly questioned him as to whether he had fought with a certain boy the night before at a big outdoor event in town. There, standing in our living room, he quietly acknowledged that he had fought the other boy. It was then that I noticed his knuckles were reddened.

The police officer instructed me to drive down to the police station and bring John along. There at the station, another officer spoke with both of us, clearly stating that, according to the report he had received, John had provoked the fight. The result was that the other boy had been badly beaten up. John just sat there staring, occasionally admitting his actions. All of this was written up as the officer warned him not to let this ever happen again, as an assault charge was not something to look upon lightly. Apparently the other boy's parents, while upset, were not ready to press any charges. Not *yet*, anyway.

The warning was sobering enough that, along with the trip to the police station, we hoped John had learned his lesson. Sadly, such was not to be the case. Little did I know it at the time, but John had not only started the fight but blindsided the other boy, so that it was not a "fair fight." The whole thing had started because the boy had made a pass at John's girlfriend. I spoke to

John seriously about the potential ramifications of his actions, but he remained almost brazen, not even relieved that he'd gotten out of what could have been a real legal mess for him.

Then, less than two weeks later, it happened again. Same outburst. Same reason. Different kid. This time it happened at the high school during a sporting event. Except this time John picked on someone *not* his own size—a bigger kid who chose to fight back. John popped him, and the other kid popped him right back, giving him a badly swollen eye. Someone alerted the campus police officer, while John, knowing that he was facing trouble, fled the scene.

Meanwhile, I was in the middle of a church revitalization meeting in a local restaurant with our group of church planters and leaders from another church who were asking us to come in and take over their church in order to revive it. All very noble and exciting. We had barely begun our meeting when my phone rang. It was the principal. I never did welcome his phone calls and, admittedly, sometimes deliberately ignored them. I knew that this time I couldn't ignore the call, given what John had just been through and the alarming fact that it was already 7:30 p.m. Though the principal called often, he rarely called me except during school hours, so I knew this must be serious.

It was. I walked away to take the call.

Standing outside the restaurant, I listened to what had happened, how John had fled the scene and that the school had had no other choice but to notify the local law enforcement. Then, to add insult to injury, he told me that John was hereby expelled from school and would not be allowed to return. Stunned, though not shocked, I understood the frustrated principal's words and didn't resist them. John had pulled his last straw. Nevertheless, my fatherly instincts were simultaneously firing on all cylinders. How was John? *Where* was John?

I called him repeatedly, but he wasn't receiving or returning my calls. I went home to inform my wife what was happening. As I was explaining to her what had happened, a policeman arrived at our home. He kindly informed us that they, too, were looking for him and instructed us to notify them as soon as we heard from him.

It would turn out to be a very long night.

No John.

No word.

No knowledge of where he might be.

Nothing.

Late the next morning, John returned home. He walked into the house as though he had just returned from a nice walk or something. No word or explanation. His face was swollen and his eye bruised. He looked somewhat sheepish, as though realizing that the tables had been turned on him, but he was hardly humble. We sat and talked. I told him of the call from the principal and the visit from law enforcement. He understood that we had no choice but to go to the sheriff's station as we had been instructed.

When we arrived, we informed the person at the desk who we were and that we had been asked to come in. The next scene will forever be tattooed in my mind. The officer, having looked up whatever information was on his computer, calmly walked around the counter and asked John to turn around and put his hands behind his back. Right there, in front of me, he handcuffed my 16-year-old son, walked him outside, and placed him in the backseat of a police vehicle. He looked back at me and told me that John was now under arrest and would be taken to the juvenile detention center, where he would remain for the next two weeks. I remember the feeling of being gutted on the spot as he drove off with John in the backseat. For the first time in my life, I had no control, no say, over my own son. He was quite literally in the hands of another authority—this one not so forgiving. He was under arrest for assault and battery. And, yes, the former incident was back on the table.

> FOR THE FIRST TIME IN MY LIFE, I HAD NO CONTROL, NO SAY, OVER MY OWN SON.

For the first time in my life, I had to lawyer up. An attorney from our church agreed to take up the matter pro bono, which was very kind. All John had going for him was his age and immaturity. Otherwise, he was dead-to-rights guilty. And guilty he was pronounced as he stood in shackles before a judge. As he arrived in court, I walked up to hug him, but he didn't want to be hugged, nor did the guard want me hugging him.

It was all so heart-wrenching.

In the end, John was released into our custody. For the next several months he would have to wear an ankle bracelet and stay relatively close to home. Over time and following good behavior, they removed the locator but sternly warned him that, if he had even one more incident, he would not go to juvenile but, instead, adult jail—into the system that was swallowing up so many other young men.

Having been kicked out of high school, John was now in an alternative school for kids like him. For a while, he was advancing without any real problems. To no one's surprise, however, he began to push his luck, staying out later and later. Then one night he didn't come home. That was the night that would change me forever. My dark night of the soul.

MY IDOL REVEALED

It was a Saturday night. During those days John was usually back home before midnight, but it was now past 1:00 a.m. and he was still gone. It was not unusual for me to go to bed after that time on Saturdays, but now I was starting to get worried. Once again, he wasn't answering calls or texts. I knew he was probably up to no good, but where would it lead? As my anxiety mounted, I found myself sick with worry. *Is this it? Is this where he gets arrested again and thrown into real jail?* It was now after 2:00 a.m. and still no word. Finally, I went to bed. My wife was already asleep, so I wasn't about to burden her by sharing the situation. As I lay there in bed, I began to plead with God. I cried out to Him that He would have mercy on John's soul and cause him to repent of his sin and rebellion. "Oh God, please! I beg You, save John from his sins and make him Your child!" I cried quietly.

Suddenly and inexplicably, God spoke to me in my anguish. I didn't hear a voice but somehow heard Him speak directly to my heart: "Look at you. You're not trusting Me in this." I was in shock. But God was still speaking. "You tell everyone else to trust Me, but here you are in a state of despair." I spoke back to God:

"Lord, I do trust You . . ."

God cut me off in mid-sentence:

"No, you don't."

"Yes, I do."

"No—you don't."

"But, Lord, I do trust You."

"*NO*—you don't! In fact, you've made John into an idol. You're more concerned over his soul than you are in honoring Me."

That got my attention. It was then that I sensed the Lord asking me the hardest thing I have ever been asked: "Pat, will you choose to honor Me even if I don't save your son? Will you love Me more than the life and destiny of your own son?"

That broke me.

The truth I had shared with the young widower months earlier came to my mind: "Because your steadfast love is better than life, my lips will praise you" (Psalm 63:3).

> I SENSED THE LORD ASKING ME THE HARDEST THING I HAVE EVER BEEN ASKED: "PAT, WILL YOU CHOOSE TO HONOR ME EVEN IF I DON'T SAVE YOUR SON? WILL YOU LOVE ME MORE THAN THE LIFE AND DESTINY OF YOUR OWN SON?"

God's love was better than life its very self. That meant better than John's life as well. In that moment, lying on my bed of tears, the Lord revealed to me that what was happening to John was not as much about John as it was about *me.*

I'm not Job. I wasn't satanically stricken with sores. I didn't have three friends rubbing into my face their distorted versions of God's disciplinary action against me. I didn't see a whirlwind. I didn't hear the audible voice of God. I wasn't given a lesson on God's creative powers to make me feel like the speck of dusk that I am and to which I will one day return. My sufferings were minuscule compared to those of this early patriarch in the faith. But I did hear from God. I did repent—and I was to be restored in that very moment.

In that moment I openly (though quietly) wept. God had confronted me on my idolatry, and I was just as guilty as my son had been before a much lesser judge. I asked God to forgive me. Then, swallowing hard, I went on to declare, "Lord, I do love You, and I will honor You more than the soul of my own son. You alone are worthy of such attention and passion—attention and passion I have been withholding from you but giving to my son. From now on, I will trust You. I will rest in You. And I will live for You—You, Who are better than life itself—regardless of what happens to John."

My prayer was one of repentance and faith. In the moment I felt the same way I had the night I had placed my faith in Jesus to save me nearly thirty years earlier. And, as then, I was freed. I felt a peace come over me that I had not experienced since the day I had been saved from my sins. That night, I again was saved. Saved, that is, from the burden, the worry, the *idol* of putting my son's salvation and life over my love for God.

In seconds, I was fast asleep.

As a test of my sincerity, things got worse in John's life before they got better. A lot worse. He never did come home that night, and he came dangerously close to being rearrested and sent to adult jail. His actions that followed would continue to be of great concern to his mother and me. But there was one huge difference: I was free. John was no longer my idol. I could no more control his destiny than I could control the wind. I had peace and was content to wait upon the Lord to change the heart of my son. And, wouldn't you know it—He did!

But that's another story.

CULTIVATING HUMILITY

Because your steadfast love is better than life, my lips will praise you (Psalm 63:3).

Do you believe that? Is God's lovingkindness *really* better than life itself?

For God's lovingkindness to become better than life itself, some things in life must die. The first is self. When God asked Abraham to sacrifice his son Isaac, Abraham probably died a number of "deaths" leading up to the moment he wielded a knife over Isaac on Mount Moriah. But in that moment, he truly died to himself. Note the very words of God's angel to Abraham as he stopped him from actually killing Isaac: "'Do not lay your hand on the boy or do anything to him, for now *I know that you fear God*, seeing you have not withheld your son, your only son, from me'" (Genesis 22:12, emphasis mine). In that moment Abraham proved that his love and devotion to God far surpassed his love for his one and only son. By the way, we would do well to remind ourselves that what God asked Abraham to do was exactly what He Himself would do—offer up His Son as a sacrifice.

Hard as it might be to die to oneself, God cares because God knows. He knows the pain. He knows the sacrifice. He knows the loss—your loss. No one has sacrificed more than God Who gave His one and only Son for us.

Is God challenging you with a person or thing that might have become an idol to you? Will you declare to God that His lovingkindness is better than life itself? Will you then make your lips praise Him? Are you able to say to God, "Lord, I choose to love you more than _____" (Fill in the blank). Now, are you willing to surrender it—*them*—to God?

SCRIPTURES FOR MEDITATION

Genesis 22; Psalm 63:3; Luke 14:26–27; Roman 12:1–2

CHAPTER 10

PATHS LEAD TO PLACES

I have taught you the way of wisdom;
I have led you in the paths of uprightness.

PROVERBS 4:11

Many years ago I received a phone call from a business where one of our church members worked. This man had been caught viewing homosexual pornography during business hours on a company computer. He was highly valued, and the company's manager reached out to me for help; I was more than willing.

This church member was also my friend. He loved the Lord and had a godly wife and a beautiful family. I felt anxious to help him but not sure where to start, so I simply asked him to tell me his story. As it turned out, it was not unfamiliar—he had been sexually abused as a child by a trusted friend of the family and had become sexually confused. By the time he reached adulthood, he had demonstrated effeminate characteristics. Still, he fell in love with a beautiful, Christ-honoring woman, got married, and started a family. Sadly, this story has been played many times. As I listened, I wondered how to counsel him beyond the basics: confess your sin, turn from your sin, seek forgiveness from those you've hurt, read God's Word, and become accountable.

My friend had struggled with sexual temptation for years; he had also experienced real victory over the years. During his walk with Jesus, he had successfully overcome his battle with same-sex attraction. He loved and enjoyed his wife and faithfully served the Lord in the church.

So, what had happened? Where did he fall? *When* did he fall? His answers to those questions immediately drew my mind to Solomon's repeated warnings in the book of Proverbs regarding the *paths* we take. As he shared his story, my friend told of one particular night when he had "ended up" in a gay bar. From there, he said, "Things just got worse."

My mind focused on the line "I ended up in a gay bar," so I simply asked him, "*How* did you end up in a gay bar?" I could tell he really hadn't thought about that question. He went on to say that, as he drove through town, he felt drawn to the area where the bar was located, and he knew the type of bar it was. Suddenly, the point of so many biblical Proverbs hit home like a sledgehammer.

"You didn't just end up there," I said. "You had to drive there. You had to take the *path* that led to the bar. In fact, you had to *think* about driving there before you got in your car to drive into that area."

He nodded along in agreement as I laid out his path. I went on to point out the many proverbs that speak of the *path*. In that moment, the Lord seemed to give me a truism: *Paths lead to places.* My friend had lost the battle in his mind (where all paths begin) before he had driven his car like a lamb to the slaughter to the place of moral compromise.

PATHS LEAD TO PLACES

Often those who fall into sin refer to "the place they ended up" as though that destination magically and mysteriously appeared before them. But that is never what happens. There is always a path that leads to a place. And it's on that path that our battles are won or lost.

THERE IS ALWAYS A PATH THAT LEADS TO A PLACE. AND IT'S ON THAT PATH THAT OUR BATTLES ARE WON OR LOST.

I've coined a handful of phrases in my life as a biblical communicator, but none has been referred to and quoted by others as often this one: *Paths lead to places.* That expression is a virtual summary of many of Solomon's proverbs:

> "My son, do not walk in the way with them; hold back your foot from their paths" (Proverbs 1:15).

> ". . . men with perverted speech, who forsake the paths of uprightness to walk in the ways of darkness" (Proverbs 2:13).

> "Her house sinks down to death, and her paths to the departed; none who go to her come back, nor do they regain the paths of life. So you will walk in the way of the good and keep to the paths of the righteous" (Proverbs 2:18–20).

> "I have taught you the way of wisdom; I have led you in the paths of uprightness" (Proverbs 4:11).

"Ponder the path of your feet; then all your ways will be sure" (Proverbs 4:26).

"A man's ways are before the eyes of the LORD, and he ponders all his paths" (Proverbs 5:21).

"I have perceived among the youths, a young man lacking sense, passing along the street near her corner taking the road to her house" (Proverbs 7:8).

"Let not your heart turn aside to her ways; do not stray into her paths" (Proverbs 7:25).

"In all your ways acknowledge him, and he will make straight your paths" (Proverbs 3:6).

An important note: the path per se is not always an evil one, as the expression "paths lead to places" might seem to imply. At least four of the passages above express *positive* results from simply following the right path. Take the words of Solomon to his son in Proverbs 4:11: "I have taught you in the way of wisdom; I have led you in the paths of uprightness." I often tell parents that they can all tell their children one day "I have taught you" and "I have led you." But only the wise can say "I have taught you in the way of wisdom," and only the righteous can say "I have led you in right paths."

In other words, the paths we take and the paths we point others toward contain both positive and negative ramifications. In Galatians 6:7–8 Paul gives a New Testament parallel: "Do not be deceived: God is not mocked, for whatever one sows, that will he also reap. For the one who sows to his own flesh will from the flesh reap corruption, but the one who sows to the Spirit will from the Spirit reap eternal life." The metaphor there, of course, is *sowing and reaping*, whereas in Proverbs the metaphor is the *path*.

I'm purposely including the paths toward which we point others because this truth resonated most deeply with me in yet another story of retraction.

Earlier, I wrote of the extrabiblical position I had once taken on music. That wasn't the only extrabiblical position I had held. I actually had a short *list* of things I once believed and declared but have since retracted. In the process of retracting, I had to acknowledge to my congregation that I had gone too far on some issues. One huge issue came to light; although not a doctrinal position per se, the issue evoked (and still evokes!) deep passions and powerful emotions in many—especially those directly and negatively impacted by divorce and remarriage.

IN MANY CASES SCRIPTURE IS NOT AS DOGMATIC AS WE MIGHT THINK.

On that subject, I had taken my congregation down (what I now understand to be) an unbiblical path in my teaching. Substituting the more honest term "unbiblical" for the softer "extrabiblical" does a better job of raising an alarm. When we go beyond the Bible, we are in a sense refuting the Word of God. We should all be leery of going beyond Scripture on anything we believe. However, when we identify things as unbiblical that are truly unbiblical, we are simply being honest.

On the issue of divorce and remarriage, I had led my people along an intolerant path that had led to a fixed place. Let me be quick to say that the purpose of this section is not to change your thinking on marriage and divorce. Rather, it is to get you to think through and perhaps rethink your position on things. In many cases Scripture is not as *dogmatic* as we might think.

I still remember the day I publicly changed my position on marriage and divorce. After months of personal study, I planned to retract my former position and teach my new position directly from the Bible (as I understood it) before the members of my church. Knowing this could potentially be an explosive issue, I purposely segregated all the kids from the teaching time by addressing it during adult Sunday school. I had taught Sunday school before preaching the morning worship service many times before, but this was the first time I had prepared more thoroughly for Sunday school than for my message.

That morning in Sunday school I brought this opening thought to the adults: "Most people want their pastor to be like Jesus—the same yesterday, today, and forever." I wasn't attempting to be cute or clever. I was simply stating an objective truth. While most Christians would agree that every Christian—including pastors—should always be growing, repenting of misinformed beliefs and unhelpful behaviors and therefore changing throughout life, change can be unsettling—especially when it comes to one's own pastor. The pastor helps keep the church steady. His presence, his strength during times of crisis, his consistency in an ever-changing culture, and his dedication to the Word of God through it all gives security to the flock. But the truth is that pastors change. That includes, from time to time, our understanding of particular doctrines, practices, and controversial issues that the Bible might not address with absolute clarity. The very reason marriage, divorce, and remarriage have been so debated is that there is no absolute biblical clarity on the subjects. At stake is that one's position on this and other issues goes on to become one's path.

And paths lead to places.

By starting out that morning with the statement "Most people want their pastor to be like Jesus—the same yesterday, today, and forever," I set myself up to teach about the progression in my belief on the issues of marriage and divorce. Of course, it's one thing to change methodology but quite another to rethink a belief or biblical position on a controversial issue. And divorce and remarriage were definitely controversial issues.

I started by acknowledging my former position of no divorce/no remarriage, a position I had both taught and preached from that very podium. I was now about to teach otherwise. I explained that I had previously taken my cues (path) from two highly respected sources: one a former pastor and the other a nationally known teacher of biblical life principles. I'd had profound respect for this teacher—possibly too profound.

I told the class members that I had decided to do something novel—study the subject myself! I confessed that, during my renewed study, I had come to realize that I had based my "conviction" on divorce and remarriage not as much on the Bible as on those two respected but extrabiblical sources. I do believe that those teachers based their own convictions on Scripture. But, to my shame, I had based my convictions on *their* convictions! As such, I was leading my own people down a *secondary path* from the Word of God itself.

Beginning with that confession, I taught those precious saints what I had learned from my study of Scripture on divorce and remarriage. The point here is not whether I am correct in my conclusions, nor does it have to do with how convincingly I addressed the church members. The point is that I retracted—repented, even—from having taken a path of supposed truth laid out by *men* and not by God's Word. I can still see Stacey, a young wife and mother, who normally looked up joyfully as she heard the truth coming from the pulpit. Now she stared up with what appeared to me to be something like cynicism. And who could blame her? Previously, I had taught her and the whole congregation on this topic with equal conviction but from a very different point of view. In fact, my assistant, who had recently joined the staff, discovered a tape of me preaching years earlier on marriage and divorce. I asked him, "What did you think?" His reply: "Very convincing!"

So, there was that.

In that past message, however, I had neglected to tell my people how I had overlaid the text of Scripture with what I had drawn from those two huge influencers in my life. Was I being dishonest back then? No. But I had been one or two clicks away from the Word of God—a very weak and potentially dangerous place to be.

One of my sons, now in ministry, is a huge C. S. Lewis fan. For a time it seemed as though he was more apt to quote the great thinker-novelist-writer-theologian than the Bible itself. I joked with my son that, if he kept it up, I was going to start calling him "One-click Johnny" because every time he based a truth on another human he was one click away from the truth of God. The exhortation stuck. He still loves Lewis but has come to love God's Word first.

So, if paths lead to places, and they do, to what place had my position (path) in this situation—no divorce and no remarriage under any circumstances—taken me and the church I pastored? It grieves my heart to acknowledge that my belief at that time meant that every divorced man or woman was forever stuck, never to know the joy of remarriage. It meant that a divorced member would be forever consigned to the position of "that" person—the one who, while a child of God, would for their remaining days on earth be "less than" the rest of us. In that church, a divorced person would never be given an opportunity to teach the Bible—not even to children. And don't even think about becoming a deacon, much less considering ministry. This *path* of no divorce or remarriage under any circumstances (other than bereavement) led to the *place* of spiritual disablement for those suffering such circumstances. Ball-and-chained "until death did they part" this world.

The change in my position on the subject did not—at least not right away—produce any change in practice at this country church. However, this new understanding did open a whole new world of service for some in my next pastorate.

The retraction that grew out of my study: with God's help, I would not base my convictions on the words of people but on the truth of God, as the Spirit of God led me. This is not to say that we may ignore our pastors and teachers. Scripture is clear on the role of teachers in our lives and on the attention, respect, and obedience we are to give them (Ephesians 4:11–14; Hebrews 13:17). It is to say that we must never become so enamored of them or their positions on controversial matters that we forget that their job is to communicate what God's Word teaches, not their own opinions.

CULTIVATING HUMILITY

The principle that "paths lead to places" works both positively and negatively. If you're on a path of sin, know this: the fun, like a rollercoaster ride, will be short-lived. But, unlike the case with a rollercoaster, the sudden stop at the end of the path will almost always be in a bad place. *The key is to recognize the path you are on while you are on it.* It has a destination—an ending place—and, if it's not a good one, it's time to get off that path!

Even your theological and moral beliefs have taken a *path* to arrive at their current point. Some paths include the influence of our parents; friends; churches; respected speakers; and the schools we attend. Each influencer, though likely well-intentioned, might not have taken a biblically accurate stance. Stop for a moment and ask yourself, *Why do I believe what I believe?* That is the exact question I asked myself before I became a Christian. The answer led me to think for the first time in my life beyond the confines of my spiritual upbringing and put me on a biblical path that led to a transforming place.

Scripture alone should be our standard of right and wrong. When Scripture does reveal that someone has led you down a path not of God, turn back. Perhaps the prophet Jeremiah put it best: "Thus says the Lord: 'Stand by the roads, and look, and ask for the ancient paths, where the good way is; and walk in it, and find rest for your souls'" (Jeremiah 6:16).

Read Revelation 2:1–7. In this passage Jesus addressed the church in Ephesus; Paul had written a letter to the same church some thirty years earlier. The believers had so much going for them, but they had lost their first love. Jesus pointed out that the path they took had led them to a place that threatened to extinguish the church's very existence. The Lord gave powerful and concise counsel: "Remember therefore from where you have fallen; repent and do the works you did at first. If not, I will come to you and remove your lampstand from its place, unless you repent" (Revelation 2:5).

Think upon Jesus's simple outline:
1.   Remember
2.   Repent
3.   Repeat

Remember *from where you have fallen.* Recall the time you stepped onto the path that led to this place—in the case of the Ephesians, the place of lost love.

Repent. Repentance is the change in your thinking that leads away from the bad place to a new path leading to a good place. (And if the place is good, the path that takes you there will be, too!)

Repeat. (*Do the works you did at first.*) How wonderful to know that Jesus isn't asking you to reinvent the wheel. Jesus gave the Ephesians this refreshing truth: If it worked before, it will work again! As Jeremiah said, "Ask for the ancient paths, where the good way is; and walk in it." In other words, get back on that good path!

Happy travels.

SCRIPTURES FOR MEDITATION

The book of Proverbs, noting its emphasis on the path; Isaiah 8:20; 1 Thessalonians 5:21; 2 Timothy 3:16-17; 1 John 4:1

CHAPTER 11

GRAYING IN GRACE

I have been young, and am now old . . .

PSALM 37:25

am now old enough to have traveled a few roads, and I can look back at more than a snapshot or two of my life. In the words of an old preacher, "I'm not at the finish line yet, but I can see it from here."

Isn't it interesting that the preachers and authors many young believers (and preachers) clamor after are often young themselves? I find that curious. Granted, some of these men are incredibly gifted and blessed by God. I'm not suggesting that we ignore their message. I have been personally challenged by some of the outstanding writings of young, visionary, and spiritually adept men. Yet are we to think these youngsters carry the sum of all wisdom in our age? I think not. I hope not! These young talents have barely seen the ink dry on their seminary degrees, much less have the perspective that time + experience + sorrow + pain + victory + loss + seeing God through it all will teach them.

But King David had that perspective.

One day in his later years, he paused in his songwriting and lifted his quill as flashes of his past flooded in: shepherding as a boy, battling with wolves and bears, being anointed king by Samuel, slaying Goliath, singing songs of praise and struggle, running from Saul, hiding in caves, providing for six hundred men while living in those caves, ascending to the throne, fighting wars, experiencing victories, committing adultery with Bathsheba, ordering murder, repenting, grieving the betrayal of a son, holding onto the promises from God, and so much more. All of this may have been going through his head when, by the inspiration of the Holy Spirit, he bent over his papyrus and wrote; "I have been young, and now am old, yet I have not seen the righteous forsaken or his children begging for bread" (Psalm 37:25).

I have always been captivated by that reflection from David. Here was a man writing from the perspective of an entire lifetime filled with experiences, both good and bad. That line is full of implication. It suggests, "Listen to me! I'm not speculating about life, and I'm not impersonating a perfect man. I'm *communicating* what I've learned from a life lived—not always well, but *lived*. I've earned your audience, so please lend me your ear."

Think about it. David could not have written those words while enduring ten years on the run from Saul. He was still young and, fortunately, very fast! When you read Psalm 13 or similar psalms written during his times of running, David seems not to be trusting but *wondering*, and at times even *doubting*, whether God would come through. He simply could not have written "I have been young, and now am old" when he was young. Only with the graying hair of age and experience could he have penned those words.

Augustine is a name familiar to most of us. Catholics and Protestants alike love him and claim him as one of their own. This brilliant theologian wrote his *Confessions* at only 26 years of age. Twenty-six! That seems crazy to us, but it's true. Many young seminary students are well aware that Augustine penned this great theological work at such an early age. What they may not know is that Augustine also wrote another book when he was 72 and called it *Retractions* (my inspiration for this book). In this work, he took the time to correct some errors from the writings of his youth. As he looked back on his life's work, captured in writing, he noted places at which he had changed his mind, pointing out passages where he had erred. Interestingly, one Augustinian scholar writes, "The older Augustine writing his Retractions was no longer as confident in the matter as had been the younger Augustine when writing so many decades previously."[7] In other words, time had tempered the elder saint; no doubt he walked as a much humbler man at that later time.

As a young follower of Jesus, I portrayed a man on fire for God, boldly going where few are willing to go. If I saw error, I rarely missed an opportunity to confront it. After all, Solomon had written, "Those who . . . keep the law strive against [the wicked]" (Proverbs 28:4). I debated rabbis, evolutionists, Arminians, Charismatics, and even liberal pastors. I once confronted a pastor after he'd performed the wedding of a friend of mine. In his challenge to the couple, he had actually called the apostle Paul a chauvinist. I was beside myself, . . . and soon after I was beside *him*—addressing his outrageous comments. I loved verses like "Let the high praises of God be in their throats and two-edged swords in their hands" (Psalm 149:6). I once heard the old Baptist preacher Oliver B. Green quote that verse and declare: "Praise the Lord while you're cuttin' 'em down with the Word!" That's what I did. And, to my shame, I loved it.

Yikes.

But then something normal, natural, and very helpful happened. I got older. Of course, as I did I experienced many of the ups and downs of life referred to earlier. Thankfully, by God's kind grace, with every hard experience I discovered a softening in myself. How sad that *softness* is often equated with compromise. That can be the case at times, but not always. As God has softened me through the aging process, I cannot think of one core doctrinal position I have changed. Yet, I *have* changed. I've changed from having a prideful attitude with regard to those who don't see things as I do to having a respectful attitude without changing what I believe. Some of the hills I had claimed I would die on no longer exist. Those former hills today look and feel more like bumps on the road.

> BUT THEN SOMETHING NORMAL, NATURAL, AND VERY HELPFUL HAPPENED. I GOT OLDER.

Warren Wiersbe, in his autobiography *Be Myself*, includes a tremendous article he wrote in 1982 for *Christianity Today*, titled "Midlife crisis? Bah, Humbug!" He was in his fifties when he wrote it. Looking back at thirty years of serving Jesus, he wrote,

I am not as critical as I used to be, not because my standards are lower, but because my sight is clearer. What I thought were blemishes in others have turned out to be scars. In my earlier years, I was one of the six blind men describing the elephant. Today I can see the elephant clearer and also the other five men.[8]

The little church I first pastored had a group of older folks who, I later realized, were giants of the faith. They were both solid *and* sweet. In fact, one man who became like a father to me lived by this motto: "Always be sweet."

That phrase may sound mushy, but Dallas Campbell was not a mushy man. Dallas lived as a man of great conviction, which made his motto for life so powerful. He had convictions about nearly everything, doctrinal and practical. Among them: pastors should always wear a suit and only white shirts in the church pulpit; women should wear a dress or long skirt. Then, of course, there was the King James Bible. He had so many extrabiblical convictions one would think he would be impossible to be around, but just the opposite was true. He was always kind. Always amiable. Always a gentleman. Always desiring to please God—right down to his polished shoes. He truly was *always sweet,* and very dear to my heart, not because of his many convictions (some of them actually made me laugh) but because he taught me as a young man how to gray in grace.

> IT ALWAYS SADDENS ME TO TALK TO AN OLDER PERSON, A CHRISTIAN FOR MANY YEARS, WHO IS BOTH GRAY AND GRACELESS.

Charles Spurgeon once warned, "What young men are, old men will be."[9] We've all met old guys who never grew up. Men and women whose rotten attitudes from youth remain rotten when they're old. The only difference is that their rottenness smells even worse when they are older. It always saddens me to talk to an older person, a Christian for many years, who is both gray and graceless. They have resisted God's sanctifying measures in their lives. When they age, they become cantankerous. The life experiences of those who gray in grace and those who don't are those of every human. On some level, all fall on hard times: struggles with kids and losses of health, wealth, marriages, and families. They all experience trials, both of their own making and those beyond their control. The big difference between the two is fairly simple: one has learned how to gray in grace, while the other has not.

As I have shared earlier, as a young pastor I took a strong position on music. Strong, as in legalistically strong. I recall once overseeing a youth skating event involving several churches. One of the families from another church submitted Christian rock music to play as the kids skated. When I heard the music—music we wouldn't let our kids listen to, much less skate to—I had to put a stop to it. After all, the music had a beat to it, and I knew God hated music with a beat. I promptly and boldly walked up to the DJ, applied my authoritative personality, and not only put a stop to the "bad" music but successfully superimposed my own style of music (that is, God's) over the entire event.

I failed to notice a young mother there with some very upset kids. Their music had just been hijacked, but that didn't matter. Obviously, I was the proprietor of God's music standards, and they would just have to accept them.

Fast forward five or six years. My wife Nina had passed away (I know that sounds like a leap, but hang in there with me). I later began dating a widow and quickly fell in love with her. The connection? This widow was the young mother at the skating rink I had upset with my harsh behavior years earlier. In fact, that was the *only* memory her children had of me. Suffice it to say, I had much to overcome and a lot to retract.

I had been instructed by those who taught that all rock music—secular or Christian—was the devil's music. Those who indulged in listening to such music would, I knew, eventually succumb to the evils of its roots. I'm sure some of you reading this might still say "Amen!" but I no longer believe that. The truth is that, as I studied the Scripture on the subject of music, I soon realized that I had gone too far—way too far. As with my views on marriage, divorce, and remarriage, many of my "convictions" on music, to my shame, had come from men rather than God. These views came from influential individuals who cleverly used sources outside of Scripture to prove their points. My study quickly revealed that the Bible has precious little to say about style, rhythm, and beat. In addition, it promotes movement and dance, clapping, hand raising, and other expressions of praise for congregational worship.

I must give partial credit for my retractions on music to my new wife. Yes, the woman who had so much earlier been upset about my arrogance on the subject of Christian music has influenced me. I quickly discovered in Marilyn all the fruit of the Spirit Paul spoke of in Galatians 5—fruit that a passionate Christ-follower should have, . . . and yet she loved contemporary music. And now, nearly 25 years later, she still does. The reason? It's because graying in grace has pretty much nothing to do with the style of one's music. Rather, it has everything to do with the melody in one's heart (Colossians 3:16).

Our church leaders once interviewed a couple who were seeking reinstatement as members in our church after having left in a huff several years earlier. As we ended our interview, one of the other pastors, remembering the frivolous reasons they had given for their departure years earlier, asked them to explain what had changed. Some of us had been around at that time and remembered the way they had left; it hadn't been pretty, and, suffice it to say, we were interested in their reply.

The husband simply glanced at his wife, then back again at us, and said, "We were just young and dumb back then." All our leaders immediately sensed the genuineness of their humility in that simple reply. There was no need for a lengthy explanation. Age, and all the living that had transpired since that time, had beautifully softened them. They became happy and fruitful members for many years to come.

CULTIVATING HUMILITY

How old are you right now? Thirty? Forty? Older? How much older? Sixty? Older still? How has God been actually changing *you*? Be specific. Take a few moments to consider what *beliefs* and *attitudes* have changed in you over the years. Finally, how have *age* and the experience of aging factored in to any of those changes you have made?

Your Beliefs

Name one belief, one area of Bible truth, on which your position has changed. With whom, when, and where were you when the change occurred? Did the Bible's stance on the issue enter into your change of heart and mind? How? Have you ever humbly acknowledged those changes to others? Would you consider writing or even texting a thank you to those people God used to bring about the necessary change in your beliefs?

Your Attitudes

Are there any doctrinal positions you hold that, although important to you personally, would not impact someone's eternal destiny? Has your attitude toward those with whom you disagree on this or other issues kept you from loving and recognizing them as friends in Christ? Are you still persistent in that attitude, or has graying in grace helped you see the wrongness of your conviction? I love what Rowland Hill, a Baptist pastor who lived in the nineteenth century, once wrote: "I do not desire the walls that separate Christians to be torn down; only lowered, so that we might shake hands more easily over the top of them."

Your Age
(Lessons from the Palm and Cedar Tree)

Psalm 92 uses both the palm tree and the cedar tree to illustrate the fruitful walk of one who loves the Lord and grays in grace well into his or her older years:

> The righteous flourish like the palm tree
> and grow like a cedar in Lebanon.
> They are planted in the house of the LORD;
> they flourish in the courts of our God.
> *They still bear fruit in old age*;
> they are ever full of sap and green,
> to declare that the LORD is upright;
> he is my rock, and there is no unrighteousness
> in him
> (Psalm 92:12–15 emphasis mine).

The Palm Tree
Here are a few interesting facts about the palm tree, making it an encouraging metaphor for those graying in grace:

1. The palm tree's outer condition does not affect its fruit. I've often said, "The older I get, the better I was." But Paul reminds us,

> So we do not lose heart. Though our outer self is wasting away, our inner self is being renewed day by day. For this light momentary affliction is preparing for us an eternal weight of glory beyond all comparison (2 Corinthians 4:16–17).

2. Unlike other trees, the palm tree's root system develops many branches, allowing it to survive, and even *flourish*, under difficult condition.

    Growing deep roots takes time, and the Christian who grays in grace also grows a multi-branch spiritual root system over the years that helps them persevere and even flourish in hard times. Here's how the psalmist put it:

    O God, from my youth you have taught me,
      and I still proclaim your wondrous deeds.
    So even to old age and gray hairs,
      O God, do not forsake me,
    until I proclaim your might to another generation,
      your power to all those to come
    (Psalm 71:17–18).

3. The palm tree endures storms like no other tree. In fact, it can literally flatten in the wind and then spring back! Perhaps Solomon said it best: "The righteous person falls seven times and rises again" (Proverbs 24:16).

4.   The palm tree's fruit gets sweeter as it gets older. The following words of Paul are not usually applied to graying in grace, but they could be: "I am sure of this, that he who began a good work in you will bring it to completion at the day of Jesus Christ" (Philippians 1:6).

5.   Perhaps most insightful, a palm tree that has been scarred produces sweeter fruit than one unscathed by calamity.

     My favorite word in Psalm 92:14 is "still": "They *still* bear fruit in old age." Remember the life motto of my old friend Dallas Campbell? "Always be sweet." Those who gray in grace always are.

The Cedar Tree

The cedar tree is pictured on the national flag of Lebanon and symbolizes eternity, steadiness, happiness, and prosperity.[10] When you read some of the characteristics of the majestic cedars of Lebanon, it's not surprising that God would use them to picture His graying-in-grace saints.

1.   The cedar tree is called "the king of trees." It can grow to a height of more than 120 feet. Those who gray in grace earn "a crown of glory" (Proverbs 16:31).

     As a young pastor, I often took new Christians to visit George Peterson. George, in his eighties, and physically shrinking with age, was majestic in his spiritual stature to those young Christians.

2.   The cedar tree's root system is both deep and wide. The roots can go down more than twenty feet and spread over thirty feet. No wonder the Hebrew root word for

cedar is rendered in English as "firm" and conveys the idea of strength.

The Christian who grays in grace also grows deep and wide: "Therefore, as you received Christ Jesus the Lord, so walk in him, rooted and built up in him and established in the faith, just as you were taught, abounding in thanksgiving" (Colossians 2:6–7).

3. The cedar tree is one of the world's greatest resources for building.

Even the temple in Jerusalem was built with cedar.

Many years ago, I asked the man building our deck if I needed to treat the wood so that it would last longer. He smiled and told me that no, I didn't need to worry about that. When I asked why, he responded with one word: "Cedar."

4. Cedar trees don't go dormant in winter. They can grow even in the snow.

Those who gray in grace might retire from their occupations in life, but they don't retire from life or go dormant spiritually just because they are old. Art Cross, an older saint in the church I pastor, served as a deacon, studied Scripture, and even wrote a personal commentary on Proverbs while in his nineties!

5. Older saints who gray in grace are likened not simply to a cedar but to *a cedar in Lebanon*. Interestingly, the Hebrew word for Lebanon means "whiteness," a reference to the perpetually snowcapped mountains along the eastern ridge of Lebanon, canopied with cedars.

Godly older saints with "snow on their roofs" are commended by God, Who says, "Gray hair is a crown of glory; it is gained in a righteous life" (Proverbs 16:31).

6. Finally, the cedar in Lebanon can live up to one thousand years before it dies. Hence, one of the things the cedar symbolizes is eternality.

    One of the greatest gifts to the church down through the centuries has been century-old Christians. As they gray in grace, they constantly teach us how to live and die as Christians.

    No matter how old you are, you need to keep growing. And if you grow in grace, you'll gray in grace.

SCRIPTURES FOR MEDITATION

Psalm 92:12–15; Luke 9:49–50; 2 Peter 3:18

CHAPTER 12

CULTIVATING HUMILITY AFTER HUMILIATION

Humble yourselves, therefore, under the mighty hand of God
so that at the proper time he may exalt you.

1 PETER 5:6

Not long after I became a Christian, I read this description of Moses, the man who performed stunning miracles, defeated the world's greatest empire, led God's people out of slavery, personally received the Ten Commandments, led Israel to the brink of the promised land, and spoke with God face-to-face: "Moses was very meek, more than all people who were on the face of the earth" (Numbers 12:3).

What a statement! Behold, the humblest man in all the earth! Even more interesting is the historical context of the statement. Moses's authority was being challenged by his own brother and sister, Aaron and Miriam, over his marriage to a woman from Africa. In the end, God vindicated Moses and publicly shamed his brother and sister.

Even more intriguing: Moses never attempted to exonerate himself. God exonerated Moses. Herein lies the reason for the divine commentary that described not only Moses's greatness but the extent of his humility: *God loves humility.* The purpose of this book is to help you, the reader, see the importance not only of confessing and forsaking your own sin and poor judgments in life but, after having done so, of willingly keeping on confessing them. You don't need further forgiveness, but others need further instructions and are thereby helped by your stories.

I have based this concept on David's testimony in Psalm 51 and his personal hope that sinners, having read of his confession, would also return to God. But David is only one example of those who demonstrated the importance of cultivating humility *after* humiliation. The apostle Peter, who consistently stuck his foot in his mouth as he followed Jesus, later wrote to pastors, "*You who are younger*, be subject to the elders. Clothe yourselves, all of you, with humility toward one another, for 'God opposes the proud but gives grace to the humble'" (1 Peter 5:5, emphasis mine). Who were these *younger* men to whom Peter was referring? We aren't certain, but I'd like to think they were young men who either desired to become elders or who were elders and loved the authority that came with their position. Peter, now older and having learned a few lessons in humility himself, exhorted those younger men to clothe themselves in humility.

Do you remember any of the lessons Peter learned? Here are some of his well-known lines:

- "Peter took [Jesus] aside and began to rebuke him . . . 'Far be it from you, Lord!'"
- "Even if I must die with you, I will not deny you!"
- "A curse on me if I'm lying—I don't know this man you're talking about!" (Rooster crows.)

Now a few of Jesus's responses to Peter:

- "Get behind me, Satan!"
- "Simon, Simon, Satan desires to sift you like wheat."
- "Put away your sword!"
- "If it is my will that [John] remain until I come, what is that to you? You follow me!"

Babylon Bee, a satirical Christian news website, in May 2019 posted a headline as though it were reporting on events going on in heaven. The headline read: "Apostle Peter Cringes While Reading Gospel Accounts of All the Dumb Stuff He Did." The humorous post then proceeded to describe how the other apostles in heaven were getting a laugh out of reading from the four Gospel accounts of all of Peter's blunders. All the while Peter is described as sitting by them with his face in his hands.

Hilarious!

Yet, on a serious note, even a cursory reading of 1 Peter reveals how humble Peter had become in his later years; he even alluded to some of his own blunders. In 1 Peter 2:23 he urges his readers to be like Jesus and not to retaliate when wronged. Those readers would have remembered (either through direct knowledge or word of mouth) that Peter *had* retaliated in his younger days (see John 18:10). He wrote of maintaining a "good conscience" and being "self-controlled" (1 Peter 3:16; 4:7), but readers would have recalled Peter's lack of self-control and his convicted conscience when the cock crowed after he had denied Jesus. How powerful that, as the apostle concluded his first letter to the elders of the churches, he referred to himself not as the head of the church, first among the apostles, or some other proud self-description but simply as "a fellow elder" (1 Peter 5:1). He would go on to warn the leaders that the devil, like a lion, would seek them out to devour them. Did those first-century readers remember how that very thing had happened to Peter, leading to his three denials? (See 1 Peter 5:8 and Luke 22:31.)

I'll bet they did.

Finally, as Peter finished his letter with a word of hope and encouragement to those young men, he declared, "After you have suffered a little while, the God of all grace, who has called you to his eternal glory in Christ, will himself restore, confirm, strengthen, and establish you" (1 Peter 5:10). Do you think that, as Peter wrote those words, he was thinking of his own restoration by Jesus (see John 21)?

I do.

I also believe that Peter cultivated humility *after his humiliation*, just as we should. Boxing fans will remember George Foreman, the 1973 heavyweight champion of the world. Others of us may remember him for his famous cooking grill. George threw powerful punches in the ring, and he challenged the then-undefeated world champion, Joe Frazier, to a fight—which didn't last long. Before the referee stopped the fight, Foreman had dropped Frazier to the canvas six times in less than two rounds! Avid boxing fans can still hear the voice of the commentator, Howard Cosell, ringing in their ears as he cried out repeatedly, "Down goes Frazier! Down goes Frazier! Down goes Frazier!" And so Frasier fell, in humiliating fashion. George Foreman was the new king of the ring.

About a year later, Foreman was challenged by none other than "the greatest" himself, former heavyweight champion Muhammad Ali. Except that, for most prognosticators, Ali was considered to be at the end of his career, presenting no great challenge to the new champ. In fact, many believed that Ali would be badly beaten. However, to the shock of the world, Ali not only beat Foreman but *knocked him out*, regaining his former title.

As most sports go, losers don't usually enjoy reliving their losses. They would rather glory in their past victories. George Foreman, however, was an exception. Though he had many former victories to boast over, he understood that those memories would not help him in life. Many years later, whenever he opened his laptop, his screensaver portrayed the iconic picture of his fight with *Ali*. In the picture, Foreman lay on the canvas, having just been knocked out, with the ever-boastful Ali standing over him. When asked why he would have made that humiliating picture his screensaver, he replied simply, "It keeps me humble."

That is a man who cultivated humility *after* humiliation.

The day before I wrote this chapter, a few of our church staff were talking about the unusual names parents sometimes give their kids, when one of the guys—who'd clearly been around at the time of my earlier pulpit faux pas—instinctively blurted out, "Who'd ever name their kid Jacob?!"

We all (including me!) had a good laugh.

I have my own screensavers.

Do you?

CULTIVATING HUMILITY

Scripture is clear that humility is God's highway to grace. If you believe that's true, think deeply upon the following verses and choose one to take to heart and memorize:

"Toward the scorners he is scornful, but to the humble he gives favor" (Proverbs 3:34).

"One's pride will bring him low, but he who is lowly in spirit will obtain honor" (Proverbs 29:23).

SCRIPTURE IS CLEAR THAT HUMILITY IS GOD'S HIGHWAY TO GRACE.

"For everyone who exalts himself will be humbled, and he who humbles himself will be exalted" (Luke 14:11).

"Whoever humbles himself like this child is the greatest in the kingdom of heaven" (Matthew 18:4).

"Humble yourselves, therefore, under the mighty hand of God so that at the proper time he may exalt you" (1 Peter 5:6).

"God opposes the proud but gives grace to the humble" (James 4:6).

Many books, articles, and messages have been written, taught, and preached on the subject of humility. Great things, too, have been said by humble men and women. Here are just a few of my favorite quotes:

"Do you wish people to think well of you? Don't speak well of yourself." (Pascal)

"Humility is not thinking less of yourself, it's thinking of yourself less." (C. S. Lewis)

"Humility earns the respect that pride seeks after." (Unknown)

"He that is down need fear no fall; he that is low no pride; he that is humble ever shall have God to be his guide." (John Bunyan)

I have often reminded individuals that it's one thing to be humbled but another to be humble. Humiliation is inevitable for all of us. Humility, on the other hand, is a choice. One way or another, we will all be humbled. Be it through accident, job loss, financial loss, demotion, sickness, marital failure, or just the inevitable results of aging—we *all* get humbled. Even for you who think you can somehow avoid all of life's humbling circumstances, there is the whole business of having to stand before God after this life. "For we will all stand before the judgment seat of God" (Romans 14:10).

> HUMILIATION IS INEVITABLE FOR ALL OF US. HUMILITY, ON THE OTHER HAND, IS A CHOICE.

All Christians will one day stand before Jesus. There will be no boasting on that day, except in Jesus. On that day, He will boast in the work He has done in the lives He has transformed (Ephesians 2:6–7). But we will not boast in ourselves on that day. We will all be humble before Him.

A FINAL WORD

There is another judgment some of you may well be facing. It is a much graver and awful judgment than what followers of Jesus will face. It's also one that will never end. It is a judgment at which you must stand before God and be weighed, not by the gospel you received but by the gospel you rejected. At this future judgment, it will be revealed that your name is absent from God's Book of Life. The awful result will be that you will then be cast out of God's presence for all eternity.

All because you refused to get humble when humiliated.

Dear friend, please avoid that judgment. Believe this: judgment for your sins has already taken place at the cross of Jesus Christ. Believe that He died in your place, taking upon Himself your pride, your rebellion, your sin. Believe that He rose from the dead to secure your soul's destiny and grant to you life—real, abundant, glorious, and eternal life—starting now and lasting forever. If you'll trust Him today, He will save a seat for you in heaven. "[He has] raised us up with him and seated us with him in the heavenly places in Christ Jesus" (Ephesians 2:6).

In April 2018 I purchased seats in Kansas City for a Chicago Cubs and Royals baseball game to be played on August 6. Once I purchased the tickets, those seats were mine. I had bought them. While I wasn't going to be there for another five months, they were guaranteed to be mine just the same.

When Jesus died and rose again, He "purchased" our seats in heaven. When He ascended to heaven, He was *seated* at the right hand of God (Hebrews 1:3). It is as though Jesus has gone to the game ahead of us to "save" our seats!

Much happened between April and August that year, but my seats for the game were guaranteed. Much will happen— good, bad, and otherwise—between now and heaven, but Jesus has already purchased my "ticket" and is now "saving my seat" for when I get there.

He'd love to save one for you, too.

SCRIPTURES FOR MEDITATION

Matthew 16:22, 23; 26:35; Mark 14:71; Luke 22:31;
John 18:11; 21:22

ACKNOWLEDGEMENTS

There are many people to thank for the idea and content of this book. A huge thanks to the staff at Saylorville Church who wondered if I would ever get this written. Special thanks in particular to my personal assistant, Lisa Johnson, who helped me keep my eye on the ball as lead pastor of our church. Trevor Meers, friend and former long-time editor, was the first to read my writing cover to cover. He was also the first to encourage me to carry on while sending me back to rework most of the original manuscript. Dianne and Hannah De Cleene, a delightful mother-daughter combo, together really gave this book the traction it needed through their editing skills. Their keen observations and suggestions saved me from further humiliation.

It's hard to express the depth of gratitude I have for those whose names appear in this book, and who significantly contributed to several of the retractions I record. Some of my life heroes, like Dave Leonard, Dallas Campbell, and Bill Clark, are all with Jesus today, but their impact on my life continues.

Finally, I want to thank my wife, Marilyn. Her godly life and character have helped me to cultivate humility after many humiliating experiences—one of them recorded in this book.

NOTES

1   Warren Wiersbe, *In Praise of Plodders* (Grand Rapids: Kregel, 1991), 11.

2   Readers might be aware that Augustine, the eminent church father, wrote what he called his Retractions (Latin, *Retractationes*) later in his life. In the interest of full disclosure, I did get the idea for my book title from Augustine. His Retractions, however, might be better translated "Reconsiderations." Most historians who have read or studied Augustine's retractions see them more as revisions than as outright refutations or complete turnarounds.

3   Watson F. Pindell, *Milestones to Immortality: The Pilgrimage of Abraham Lincoln* (Baltimore: Role Models, Inc, 1988), 42.

4   Peter Cozzens, *The Earth is Weeping* (New York: Random House, 2016), 245.

5   C. S. Lewis, *Mere Christianity* (New York: HarperCollins,1952), 192.

6   Walk Thru the Bible, founded by Bruce Wilkerson in 1976, is an outstanding ministry that teaches how to see the Bible from a big-picture perspective.

7   Augustine of Hippo, "2148 The Retractions," AUGNET.ORG, http://augnet.org/en/works-of-augustine/writings-of-augustine/2148-the-retractions/.

8   Warren Wiersbe, *Be Myself* (Grand Rapids: Baker Books, 1994), 274.

9   Sermon preached at Metropolitan Tabernacle. See https://www.spurgeon.org/resource-library/sermons/a-description-of-young-men-in-christ/#flipbook/.

10   "Flag of Lebanon," Wikipedia, 2022, https://en.wikipedia.org/wiki/Flag_of_Lebanon.

ABOUT THE AUTHOR

PAT NEMMERS (BA, Faith Baptist Bible College) has served as lead pastor of Saylorville Church in Des Moines, Iowa, since 1998. His focus on personal evangelism and discipleship has produced a church that continues to experience exponential growth. In addition, Pat founded the Engage Network, a church planting fellowship of seven Gospel-centered churches in the greater Des Moines area with over 4,000 people. He and his wife, Marilyn, speak at conferences across the globe. He and Marilyn were both widowed when the Lord brought them together in 1997. Together they have 10 children and over 30 grandchildren.

Made in the USA
Middletown, DE
02 January 2023

21132625R00099